TEXAS BED & BREAKFAST

TEXAS BED & BREAKFAST

YOUR COMPLETE GUIDE TO 137 BED AND BREAKFAST INNS IN MORE THAN 35 TEXAS CITIES.

BY ANN RUFF, GAIL DRAGO, AND MARJIE MUGNO

★
TexasMonthlyPress

Texas Monthly Press, Inc.
P.O. Box 1569
Austin, Texas 78767

A   B   C   D   E   F   G   H

Library of Congress Cataloging in Publication Data

Ruff, Ann, 1930–
    Texas bed & breakfasts.

    Includes index.
    1. Bed and breakfast accommodations—Texas—
Directories.   I. Drago, Gail, 1947–   .   II. Mugno,
Marjie.   III. Title.   IV.   Title: Texas bed and breakfasts.
TX907.R843   1985   647'.9476403   85–7968
ISBN 0–87719–020–8 (pbk.)

CONTENTS

ACKNOWLEDGMENTS

How can I ever thank all those delightful B&B people that I met? Not only were the hosts and hostesses all so gracious and their homes so charming that I wanted to stay in every one, but those untiring ladies who drove me around and saved me untold hours of looking for addresses deserve a special place in my heart. Laverne Campbell showed me San Antonio as I have never seen it, Helen Taylor gave me a great introduction to Fredericksburg, and Kathy Smolick conducted a super tour of the capital. Also, thank you, Kenn Knopp, for getting this whole idea started in the first place. This is going to be a wonderful book because the B&B world is so full of wonderful people.

Ann Ruff

First and foremost, I would like to thank Anthony and Nicholas Drago, Waverly Constantine, and Ruby Rawlinson for providing me with an atmosphere in which I could do my work. Thanks also go to Sylvia, Aaron, and Summer Lewallen, Dorothy Campbell and Trisha Prejean, who gave up a weekend on behalf of this project. I also owe a debt of gratitude to Nathan Crawford, Julie Farrell, and Christine Neil, who came to my rescue when I constantly called them for help.

And, of course, this project would have never been completed without the guidance of our editors, Scott Lubeck and Anne Norman, who accepted every update with patience and goodwill.

As for the B&B people, I really appreciate the kindness that was shown me during my travels. It was people like Helen and Pat Hanemann, Pat Hirshbrunner, Marguerite Swanson, and Debbie Seigel who went above and beyond the call of duty to make sure I received a clear idea of what their cities had to offer.

Last but certainly not least, I want to thank all my Alpha Xi Nu friends of Beta Sigma Phi. Your endless encouragement has been priceless. Special thanks, however, go to Kathy Henson and Marilyn Estes, who were always there when I needed them.

Gail Drago

Introduction

*I*f you are weary of the monotony of hotel and motel rooms and you want something more than a cubicle like all other cubicles, you might want to try a new phenomenon on the Texas scene—a bed and breakfast—for different and memorable lodging.

The bed and breakfast idea, affectionately nicknamed B&B, has never been a novel one to Americans traveling on a small budget in Europe. The familiar "B&B" or "Zimmer" signs promise a comfortable room in a private home, along with a morning meal. Now there is a B&B organization in practically every major city in the United States. Texas, with its tremendous tourist appeal, is also climbing on the B&B bandwagon in a big way.

What is a Texas version of B&B? A precise, all-encompassing description is impossible, for B&Bs vary from city to city and from home to home. But basically you are a paying guest in a private home, and breakfast is included with the rent. There's more, though—much more. Your room and bath will sparkle with cleanliness, and the eclectic decor will reflect the host's personality. You will be given inside tips on what to see and do and the best places to dine. Even though a B&B will never compete with a motel for convenience or a high-rise hotel for services, it is superior in terms of one significant ingredient: personal attention. In essence, B&Bs are dedicated to providing lodging with a personal touch.

What kinds of people stay in a B&B? Ruth Wilson, the author of *Bed and Breakfast Texas Style*, says, "It is the well traveled folks who are tired of hotels and motels—bankers and bank auditors, teachers, salesmen, museum lovers, honeymooners, retired people and basically people who are planners, for reservations come in as far as a year in advance. People who stay at B&Bs are highly motivated, well organized adventurers who like meeting people."

If you are a single person traveling alone, why spend a lonely evening in a strange city when you can share the warm hospitality offered by a B&B host? Honeymooners, foreigners, and senior citizens also find B&Bs delightful. A cup of tea, a glass of wine, a morning newspaper with your coffee, and the host's sincere desire to please will ensure a visit that you will remember.

If you book your stay through one of the local bed and breakfast agencies, you will be asked to fill out a questionnaire and send a deposit for the B&B that most nearly fits your preference. Contact is never made directly with the host home. Even if you become fast friends with your host, which is often the case, you are required to use the B&B organization as a reservation vehicle.

What kinds of people operate B&Bs? Actually, they come in all varieties, from young married working couples to retired government employees. Most hosts, however, are widows or retired couples who feel they still have a lot of enjoyment to share, and they are right. Hosts are usually well traveled, are good cooks, have interesting hobbies, lead active lives, are well organized, and perhaps above all, are adventurous.

You will find B&B homes that range from a modest three-bedroom bungalow to a grand mansion; some are situated in historic homes loaded with Texas historic medallions. Whether the host home was built in the 1800s or the 1980s, each offers something unique: a host who wants you to have the best time you've ever had during your visit.

A minimum continental breakfast is required at all B&Bs, but often you are treated to a table groaning with food. A three-day notice of cancellation is required, and your deposit will be refunded except for a small processing fee. Children are not always accepted, and it is a rare B&B indeed that will take pets. Many B&Bs are also very fussy about smokers, so be sure to ask.

Often the B&B society will ask you for feedback to maintain quality control. Even if a form is not provided, a brief note praising the B&B's good points would be appreciated, as would your legitimate complaints.

If you are a newcomer to bed and breakfasts, one visit may convince you that there is no other way to travel. You can then join the rest of those who are dedicated B&B guests.

Houston, the Gulf Coast, and Southeast Texas

Bellville

THE HIGH COTTON INN

*B*ellville, a sleepy little retreat called the "belle of bluebonnet country," has within its midst a stately Victorian bed and breakfast. Known for years as the Hellmuth residence, the old home was transformed in 1983 by Houstonians Anna and George Horton, who have rechristened their new home the High Cotton Inn. The main goal in their efforts to refurbish the structure was to restore its original beauty and elegance, thus preserving the Hellmuth history. The home's beginnings can be traced back to 1906, when merchant Charles W. Hellmuth built the 4,000-square-foot homestead for his wife, Emma Anna, and their eight children. The love of his family and of the good life remain evident; the very structure, with its large, accommodating rooms and balconies, giant windows, and open transoms, pulsates warmth and hospitality. Though George and Anna have added bathrooms upstairs, a sitting area, a downstairs bedroom, and a back porch that looks out over the pool, the original cypress house remains intact. Though most of the house is furnished with family antiques and decorated with period wallcoverings and accessories, the kitchen, sitting room, and bathrooms are contemporary, creating a somewhat eclectic mood.

The High Cotton Inn

The downstairs bath, part of the Hortons' private quarters, has a history all its own. This small room, which connects with the bedroom that belongs to Campbell, the Hortons' daughter, was once called the "brides' room" by the Hellmuth family. It was the custom that every one of the five sons bring his bride to the homestead for one year so her mother-in-law could teach her the art of housekeeping.

Guests sleep upstairs in one of the five bedrooms, sharing the two and a half baths and a sitting room that opens up on a veranda. Each room is named after either a relative or a friend of the Hortons, with individual motifs chosen to fit the respective personalities of the namesakes. The Jay Bute Room is named, for example, after the vice president of Bute Paint Stores in Houston, who donated paint, flooring, and wallpaper for the B&B's restoration. Because he likes duck hunting, the wallpaper in this room sports little ducks. Bobby Russell's Room is decorated with the American Indian in mind; Russell, a close friend of the Hortons who donated many weekends to the restoration project, is particularly interested in this subject. In Uncle Buster's Room—named after George's great-uncle Cleveland Sewall, after whom Rice University's Sewall Hall was christened—antique buffs will note the Victorian bed that actually belonged to this successful Houstonian. Ella Campbell's Room is decorated in pink, an appropriate color for the feminine Mrs. Campbell. The pitcher and washbasin in this room belonged to Anna's grandmother. The Sallie Sewall Room is named after George's grandmother. Be sure to see Mrs. Sewall's white beaded ball gown, displayed in the upstairs parlor. As reigning queen, she wore it to the turn-of-the-century Notsuoh Ball, held every year in Houston from 1899 to 1916 to commemorate the cotton industry. (Notsuoh is "Houston" spelled backwards.) The crocheted tablecloths and lace curtains found throughout the inn were handmade by Marietta Robinson, Anna's mother.

As for the food, you won't go hungry with Anna's traditional plantation breakfast, which includes eggs, bacon, sausage, homemade pastries and bread, and hot brandied fruit. A bedtime snack of wine, cheese, fruit, and homemade fudge is also provided. Sunday supper is available by reservation.

You'll want to soak up some local color while in Bellville, a quiet little town perfect for the visitor who is weary of rushed times. The town yields a few leisurely diversions, such as fishing in the Brazos River, or you could attend one of the frequent local fairs, festivals, or horse and cattle shows. This is hunter, jumper, quarterhorse, and thoroughbred country. Talk to Anna or George if you want to go horseback riding. They can arrange it. You can also visit the Blue Bell Creamery, the Bellville Potato Chip Factory, or spend the day at San Felipe State Park. For dinner, drive to New Ulm for a meal at the Parlour. Once an old funeral home, the restaurant and bar not only provides a meeting place for the town's one hundred German residents but is also the pride and joy of owner Alton Haverlah. You can listen to an oompah quartet while having a beer, or if you're interested in World War II, ask Alton to tell you his prisoner-of-war stories.

A weekend in Bellville will give you a chance to slow down a little and find out what it's really like to be "in high cotton."

214 S. Live Oak
Bellville 77418
(409) 865-9796
5 guest rooms, 2½ shared baths
Moderate
Children welcome, but bring
sleeping bags

Chappell Hill

BROWNING PLANTATION

*O*n the outskirts of Chappell Hill, hidden from the present by ageless cedar, pecan, and bois d'arc trees, stands the Browning Plantation. Once the social center for area society, the Greek Revival–style residence is today, as it was then, a monument to its builder, Colonel W. W. Browning. The Colonel loved his land, his family, and the South, but he was also a man of learning, so interested in education that he became president of Chappell Hill Female College and founder of Soule University, both once located in Chappell Hill. He built the plantation for his family in 1857 amidst his 2,000 cotton- and corn-yielding acres. He instructed that the home be adorned with gracious porches, verandas, and a spectacular rooftop widow's walk, to ensure that there was enough room for family and guests to sit outdoors on sultry afternoons to watch the frequent college athletic events that took place on the grounds. Historians tell us that young horsemen would engage in jousting matches by attempting to spear gold rings that hung from the trees lining the road that led to the house. The plantation was also the scene of many social events connected with the two colleges, affairs where romance flourished and where beautiful southern

Browning Plantation

belles set their sights on much more than the gold jousting rings.

This elegant bed and breakfast, however, was not only the setting for Chappell Hill's social butterflies; it also epitomized the southern way of life. Browning, the master of sixty-seven slaves who farmed the fertile fields, saw promise in the land that yielded him his fortune. Records indicate that his agricultural interests totaled $141,000 in 1860, a year before the Civil War began. He also saw promise in the state and organized the company that built the Washington County Railroad. In addition, he was involved in one of the first documented efforts to produce oil in Texas.

Colonel Browning was destined for greatness, but his Dixie heart was too loyal. Unconvinced that the South had lost in the war's final days, this entrepreneur bought his weal's worth of worthless war bonds. With the fall of the Confederacy came the Colonel's financial ruin. And with the freed slaves went his fortune, the grace and ambience that had characterized the plantation for so long, and a small part of the South. For Browning, all was lost, for he had paid the ultimate price for his loyalty: the life of his only son, a casualty listed among the Confederate dead.

The Brownings have long been gone from Chappell Hill, the remains of the old mansion virtually forgotten by man. The broken windows and doors became avenues for every woodsy creature, and a colony of raccoons began to claim it as their own. In fact, coon begat coon until the new owners called a halt to the gradual destruction.

Richard and Mildred Ganchan saw the Browning Plantation for what it was: a gold mine of history about to be lost. And it took a gold mine and three years to restore the place, with its fragile interior chimneys and original fascia boards and flooring that had to be removed carefully until the foundation work was done. However, when the original wood was being replaced to ensure authenticity, the Ganchans were faced with a major problem. Because all the wood had come from cedar trees on the property and had been cut by hand, none of the boards' thicknesses was uniform. As a result, workers had to plane the wood in order to put the pieces back together. Then, when the twelve-foot ceilings were removed, carpenters were literally showered with twenty years' worth of coon memorabilia. In addition, every window pane in the house had been broken, and the kitchen, once off to the side of the main house, had long ago been claimed by some forgotten hurricane. The Ganchans have since added a rustic kitchen with a glassed walkthrough that connects it with the main house. The *faux bois* graining, however, has been restored to its original luster and can be admired throughout the plantation. The perfect symmetrical order of the structure, with all the upstairs rooms the same in size and shape as the ones directly below, has been left intact.

There are four huge guest rooms on the second floor, each two sharing a half bath. All are decorated with Victorian furniture (some Eastlake pieces), as is the rest of the house. On the third floor, guests have use of "his" and "her" bathrooms that provide a study in contrast. (Men, yours is the one with the "mail slotted" door.) Gentleman guests can enjoy their own "bachelor bath," which would make even Hugh Hefner delight. The slanted tin ceiling, antique copper bathtub (there's also a built-in shower), and zebra-skin rug blend well to create a mood of male sensuality. Across the hall, ladies may lounge in the Ganchans' own stylized rendition of a posh New Orleans bordello, with mirrored walls, a white shag rug, and an antique claw-foot tub. Mrs. Browning would have uttered a horrified gasp, but you'll love it.

Though none is original to the home, all the furnishings, bought by the Ganchans in the United States and England, seem to fit perfectly. The decor is eclectic, with some primitive pieces giving light and informality to the Victorian atmosphere. Plantation and teaster beds are the focal points of the rooms, which are each painted in a different pastel shade. Downstairs there is a parlor, a library, and an elegant dining room with wet bar, where a full breakfast is served.

If you want to be a guest here, bring friends. The Houston-based Ganchans rent it only if all four rooms can be reserved at one time by your party. Eight people is the ideal number, though one guest room, equipped with two double beds, can accommodate an extra two people. The Browning Plantation, now on the National Register of Historic Places, can be yours for a weekend that you'll always remember. Who knows? One long, summer night, you may even see a shadowy Colonel Browning standing on the widow's walk or sitting on his beloved veranda. He'll be smiling, we're sure, happy to see his home beautiful once again and contented to know that he has not been forgotten, after all.

Rt. 1, Box 8
Chappell Hill 77426
(409) 836-6144 or (713)
626-9592
4 guest rooms, 2 shared half
baths
and two private baths (3rd floor)
Exclusive
No smoking. No children under
12. No pets

Corpus
Christi

SAND DOLLAR HOSPITALITY

*T*he Sand Dollar Hospitality, Corpus Christi's bed and breakfast association, which services visitors to this deep-water port, was born in July 1982. The idea of B&B was foreign then but gladly accepted in a convention city with a shortage of accommodations. For years, longtime residents of tropical Corpus had complained about the lack of hotels to meet the needs of the growing number of tourists. The city had lovely beaches, an abundance of fishing piers, and a picturesque harbor, as well as accessibility to Padre and Mustang Islands—all profitable calling cards that bring in much revenue each year. Yet, until recently (since the completion of two major hotels on Shoreline Boulevard), rooms were scarce.

Such was the concern of family therapist Pat Hirshbrunner when she went to visit her parents in Wisconsin two years ago. While reading a Chicago morning paper, she came across an article about Janet Remen, who with two friends had organized a bed and breakfast association in Chicago. The article included an address to which to write if anyone wished to inquire further. Pat felt that she had chanced upon her city's answer to its hotel prayer. Private residences could be opened to the public, thus providing a whole new dimension to the hospitality industry. When she returned home, she wrote to Janet, who not only answered promptly but also sent Pat the names of two other people who had expressed an interest in creating an association in Corpus Christi. It seems that Maureen Bennett, a parochial grade school principal, and her friend, Margaret McGeogh, an elementary teacher, had seen an article in a women's magazine about Janet and the Chicago organization. They too had written Janet to inquire, and the three later joined forces to create Sand Dollar Hospitality. Since that time, Maureen's professional obligations have forced her to give up her B&B duties. However, Pat and Margaret (who is an avid European traveler of English birth) are still heading the organization, which carries a variety of listings that are categorized as "economy," "moderate," and "deluxe" accommodations. Margaret's background on the European B&B circuit and Pat's efficient organizational skills have made this association one of the most successful in the state.

Corpus Christi, known as the Sparkling City by the Sea, is a sportsman's paradise. This deep-sea port, with its abundance of fishing piers, the harbor, and its close proximity to Padre Island and Mustang Island, will not only win the heart of every able-bodied angler, but will also snag sailing enthusiasts. Palm tree—dotted beaches stretch invitingly down Ocean Drive to soothe the furrowed brow and cool the tired body, challenging you to forget your troubles.

Corpus Christi (Latin for "body of Christ") provides refuge now as it did a century and a half ago, when Henry Lawrence Kinney arrived to establish a trading post. Then, in 1845 when General Zachary Taylor stopped here with his troops en route to Mexico, the army began to use Corpus Christi regularly as an army depot, until 1855, when the headquarters moved to San Antonio. But Kinney loved this coastal land and refused to let the settlement die. Gradually the population began to grow as fortune seekers assembled here to join California gold-rush expeditions and settlers came to hitch their wagons to the trains heading for Chihuahua. More people were brought in when oil was discovered west of the city. Today 240,000 people reside here, with 1,300 oil-producing wells silently pumping up Texas crude. How ironic that the dreamers of 1849 paused only briefly in Corpus Christi to organize their fruitless search for California gold! It was here in Texas all along, waiting underground to be discovered. The miners were simply fifty years too early.

Pat Hirshbrunner
and Margaret McGeogh, directors
3605 Mendenhall
Corpus Christi 78415
(512) 853-1222

Corpus Christi

DOLPHIN

*T*he Dolphin, a traditionally styled red and green home in an affluent subdivision of Corpus Christi, provides guests with a very accommodating place to rest after a long day of sightseeing in the sun. Your host and hostess, avid travelers and lively company, will tell you everything you need to know to enjoy yourself, from where to go on the islands to fish to the best places to eat. If you are politically minded, you'll love your hostess, who is intensely involved with the Republican party, and you'll enjoy conversing with your host, who is a retired officer in the Marine Corps. Their lovely home is proof of the full lives they are leading, with collectibles from all the places they have lived and visited. But the best part is that you'll be treated like a king, with breakfast being served to you in the formal dining room on the family's good china, with your coffee or tea poured from the hostess's silver tea service. The specialty of the house, served to those who stay more than one night, is fresh strawberry crêpes, complemented by homemade rolls, juice, and seasonal fruit. Note as you eat how pretty the beveled glass oval mirror looks with the gilded, flowered wallpaper.

After breakfast, have an extra cup of coffee in the formal living room of blues, golds, reds, and eggshell. A touch of the Oriental is present, with an exceptional Japanese gold-leaf screen and red Japanese desk, purchased when the couple lived in Japan. If you like more informal settings, take your cup into the family room, with its large fireplace and blue-with-brown color-coordinated furniture. The walls are covered with all types of art, from western renditions to temple rubbings to a collection of Japanese wood-block prints and silk pictures from Vietnam. The military background of the host is certainly apparent in the room, as a United States Marine Corps mantel clock ticks off the minutes and a bronzed drill instructor hat and swagger stick adorn the wall of the wet bar. The stick is particularly interesting, as it is made from the horn of a water buffalo, its silver handle carved by a Vietnamese artist.

Two bedrooms are available to guests, one with a double and the other with a queen-sized bed. The first is furnished with early 1800s American furniture. The marble-topped chest of drawers is more than a hundred years old. Notice the chess game set up here, but don't knock it over, because the host has been playing the game by mail for more than two years! The second room is decorated in lime and green with a dark flowered border that complements the decor. Of particular note is a lovely secretary that adds warmth and personality to this setting. A bath is shared by both accommodations.

If you're interested in staying here, remember that this B&B is not available on weekends. There is one thing for sure: American patriotism is alive and well here, with a plaster American bald eagle poised in flight over the front entrance, Marine Corps memorabilia everywhere, and a picture of President Reagan on the mantel. If you're not Republican, you can stay at this B&B anyway!

2 guest rooms, 1 shared bath
Moderate
No children. No pets.

BLUE HERON

*I*f your idea of comfort is relaxing your tired muscles in a giant new hot tub in your own private spa room, or lounging on a beautiful redwood deck alongside a secluded backyard pool, then the Blue Heron is the answer to your every prayer.

Your host and hostess, of French Canadian ancestry, open their hearts to you here, and for the length of your stay you will become one of the family. The parents of five grown children, they own a large, elegantly furnished 3,000-square-foot home that awaits only your presence. The couple has traveled and lived all over the world as a result of the host's past career in the military and as a helicopter test pilot. A worldly twosome by any standard, they have chosen to decorate their home to reflect their colorful past.

As you approach the front door, you'll know immediately that their love for Corpus Christi and the sea runs deep. An original Poseidon-sized sculpture of a sea shell created by an artistic daughter lies at the portal like some new-found seaside treasure. This theme of the sea shell is carried through the residence with numerous collections of shells, many of which have been made into craft pieces by the hostess herself.

The first thing you see as you enter this B&B is the massive dining room and living room combination, furnished in Danish modern and colored in yellows and whites. It opens onto the inviting kitchen. But the home's heart-beat can be felt in the breathtaking den, all glassed on one side to yield the luscious backyard with patio pool, diving board, and slide. Built-in book-cases hold German steins, family pictures, and a collection of Elvis Presley decanters. The contemporary bamboo-styled furniture upholstered in light blue, azure, and eggshell adds a coolness to the family room, which connects with a formal breakfast area. Here you'll be served a full American breakfast of bacon, eggs, and fresh peaches from the backyard tree. The hostess also serves munchies throughout the day, such as cheese balls and crackers.

After breakfast, you'll probably want to play pool in the glassed activity room with its game tables, stereo, wet bar, and fireplace. You'll discover the "good life" here as you gaze out onto the oleanders, bougainvillea, and ivy-covered fountain and bird bath that accent the backyard.

Luxury also extends to the guest rooms. The first room, decorated in greens, is equipped with a king-sized waterbed and French Provincial fur-nishings. The second also has a king-sized bed (this one is the regular kind), a color television, a desk, a chest of drawers, and a large shuttered window accented by designer wallpaper of ferns and foliage. A guest bath is shared by the two rooms. A craft room with a single bed can be used by guests if needed. This hostess provides her guests with specially wrapped soaps remi-niscent of the European tradition.

Whether you're one who relishes privacy or one who hates being alone, your desires will be respected. Don't pass up the chance to get to know these fine people, however. Their lives have been rich with experience.

2 guest rooms, 1 shared bath
Exclusive
No restrictions

EBBTIDE

*F*or a touch of the Old World, con-sider staying at the Ebbtide, the well-kept residence of an outgoing dentist and his assistant, who is also his wife. Though the home's exterior is traditional in every way, the interior furnishings reflect the elaborate taste of Louis XIV. The host and hostess have charm galore and will make you feel like the king himself. Located on the south side of the city, the Ebbtide will put you within minutes of the Bay, the Naval Air Station, and Corpus Christi State University.

As for your sleeping arrangements, take your pick of three guest rooms, the largest of which is at the back of the house and opens onto a huge game room. This secluded bedroom is the most informal of the three and is equipped with its own bath, air-conditioning, and private entrance. Shades of blue accentuate the twin beds and rattan sofa and chair.

If you have always wanted to stay at Versailles, sleeping in the second or third bedroom is the next best thing. The second guest accommodation, accented by burgundy velvet, houses a queen-sized bed and French Provincial—style furniture made in Spain. The flowered wallpaper here adds contrast, giving a more subdued quality to the queenly motif. If even this room is not as elegant as in your wildest dreams, stay in the third bedroom, colored in pink and decorated with royalty in mind. The first thing that will catch your eye is the French Provincial headboard, adorned with an actual painting in miniature. The gold and silver inlaid designs on the vanity and the gilded accessories would make even Louis content.

Once you're settled in your bedroom, you'll want to see the other collectibles found in the living and dining rooms. White and gold are the predominant colors, with inlaid wood and marble-topped furnishings that are in keeping with the regal theme. There is a life-sized portrait of the hostess's sister that warrants study.

If you really want to let your powdered wig down, join the host and hostess in the Mediterranean-style den, complete with big-screen television, or play pool in the game room that opens onto the pool and patio. This hostess will serve you a varied menu of breakfast foods, from bacon and eggs on weekends to a lighter continental fare on weekdays. Such treats as cookies and fresh-baked gingerbread are always out for guests to enjoy. Guests who stay at the Ebbtide have few restrictions, as they may smoke, use the kitchen and laundry, and bring along their children and pets.

3 bedrooms, 2 baths (1 shared)
Exclusive
No restrictions
Ask about rental of the
family motor home.

MARLIN

*B*egin the day leisurely by having a continental breakfast of rolls, fresh fruit, and coffee on a covered patio surrounded by flowers. Leafy grapevines shade you from the morning sun, while hanging baskets of begonias, ferns, and ivies give you privacy in the backyard of this B&B. Situated in a convenient Corpus Christi suburb, you'll be moments away from the beach, with Ocean Drive only ten minutes away, yet only a half mile from South Padre Island Drive, which will take you to such seaside retreats as Mustang Island, Padre Island, and Port Aransas.

The best feature of this B&B, though, is the caring, loving hostess, who will give so much of herself and her time to make your stay memorable. And her home reflects her warm personality, with Early American furniture and a decor in oranges and golds. The neat, large living area, complete with fireplace, grandfather clock, and overstuffed furniture, is a great place to visit, relax, or play the organ. Note the collectibles on the mantel, such as the quaint German steins, the antique Chinese vases that date back to the Boxer Rebellion, and the hundred-year-old clock, which has a warranty that reads, "Plymouth Hollow, Conn.—Guaranteed to be a good clock."

You will find the guest room more than adequate, with its new king-sized bed, gold padded headboard, and complementary dresser and chest of drawers. Feel free to use the stereo in this room, which is only two steps away from a private bath. The guest quarters are located at the back of the home and provide a maximum of privacy. A television is available upon request.

If you want to feel like a pampered grandchild, stay with this charming hostess. Your visit with her will be one that you will remember with fondness.

1 bedroom, 1 bath
Moderate
No smoking. No pets.

MEADOW VIEW

*I*n the center of Corpus Christi, just two minutes from South Padre Island Drive, is a contemporary B&B that offers comfort and privacy. The split bedroom arrangement assures that the guest of Meadow View can enjoy quiet times without distraction. However, if he wishes, he has free rein of the home, including the laundry room and privileges in the yellow, gold, and rust kitchen, decorated tastefully with flowered wallpaper, a white-curtained bay window, and plants galore. The attractive living area, furnished with contemporary and rattan furniture, provides a cheery spot to sit by the fireplace or enjoy the family entertainment center, which has a stereo and color television.

The guest room, with a private, color-coordinated bath nearby, is decorated in warm browns and whites. The double bed with white spread edged with brown piping, the wooden seaman's chest, and the wicker pieces add a feeling of home, while bamboo shades provide a light, pleasant atmosphere.

Ask your hostess if she will show you her private quarters, handsomely decorated with antique reproductions, a rattan headboard, and peach accessories. Her son's room is a traditional boy's room, complete with waterbed.

For this working mother, the breakfast fare is simple during the pressure-filled week: fresh fruit, English muffins, coffee, and juice. However, upon request, a full American-style breakfast is served on weekends.

1 bedroom, 1 bath
Budget
No pets

SEA BREEZE

A rather different sort of B&B exists on Corpus Christi Bay. This little cache is an apartment located so close to the water that you can pitch a seashell from the front door into the surf. The best feature of the Sea Breeze, though, is the nightly rate, which will not break the budget pocketbook. For a small fee, you can stay here on Ocean Drive, which is easily accessible to Padre Island Drive.

The Australian-born hostess of this B&B, a nurse and mother of a small child, provides a full Texas-style breakfast upon request; but the usual fare includes fresh fruit, cereal, sweet rolls, juice, and coffee. She will also provide interesting conversation if you wish, as she is well traveled and very familiar with the European B&B amenities.

The accommodations include a queen-sized sleeper sofa; if you bring children along, you'll need to provide bedrolls. There is one full bath shared by all. Guests may use the kitchen and living area, where they can watch television. Pool privileges are available, as long as the hostess accompanies you to the complex's facility. You may also use the coin-operated laundry.

If you decide to stay at the Sea Breeze, bring your rod and reel. There's a lighted fishing pier within a block of the apartment. But remember to arrive before 9 P.M.

1 bedroom, 1 shared bath
Budget
No pets

SEAGULL

T he Seagull, a modest yellow and white frame house on a corner in one of Corpus Christi's older neighborhoods, is only a few blocks from the Bay and very near Spohn Hospital.

While you stay there, the hostess, a world traveler who is no stranger to Europe and the Middle East, will provide you with your every need. In addition, she will tell you stories of her travels and will show you her collectibles from all over the world. (Ask to see her root collection from the Dead Sea.) However, privacy is available if you wish it, with two guest rooms that have their own entrances.

The front room was decorated with summer in mind, with a light gold carpet, a royal-blue stuffed chair, and a cheery rose, pink, and white flowered bedspread. You get a feeling of this hospitable lady's background when you see the antique sewing machine, the bookcase filled with books on every subject, and the desk full of framed pictures of her family. The second guest room, done in tan and white, has the added features of a private entrance, a vanity with sink separate from the enclosed toilet, and large shuttered double windows. The double bed is the focal point, with its contemporary spread of browns and tans, giving the feel of an Indian motif.

A third large room, once a garage and in the process of being remodeled at this writing, is available for extended periods. There is a double bed and a shower. The rest of the house, open to guests, is full of pieces of art, figurines, and other collectibles from this hostess's travels. Be sure to notice the two pictures in the living room, one of which is made of seeds from the Sea of Tiberius and the other from Scottish heather.

You have laundry privileges here, and there is bus service nearby.

**2 rooms, 1 with private
bath and 1 shared
Moderate
Smoking in limited areas. No
children under 12. No pets.**

SEA URCHIN

*L*ocated in the northwest part of Corpus Christi, the Sea Urchin sits in a new subdivision that has sprung up near the United States Naval Air Station. The mood that emanates from this family B&B is one of togetherness. Guests have full use of the house, with no restrictions other than being asked to smoke only in certain areas. Children and pets are allowed and are welcome to play with the two children and the family dog, Bingo. There are two guest rooms, with one bath shared with the family.

Both bedrooms (they second as the children's rooms) are spacious and are located close to the bath. The first room has one double and one single bed, white French Provincial furniture, and a wicker rocker. The second bedroom, decorated in brown and maroon, has twin beds and a Mediterranean oak double dresser and bureau.

If you like to play the organ, there is a small one in the formal living room; if you just like to watch television, you may join the family in the den, complete with fireplace and brown contemporary furniture. If you feel like exercise, you can work out on the gym equipment in the recreation room (converted garage) or play a game of pool with the host.

From her traditional kitchen, the working hostess serves a continental breakfast that includes cereal, toast, orange juice, and coffee. On weekends, however, she frequently serves a Mexican breakfast of tortillas, beans, eggs any style, chorizo (Mexican sausage), "south of the border" hash browns, and hot sauce.

She is a social worker, and her husband is an aircraft mechanic at the Army depot. You'll be able to practice your Spanish, as the family is fluent in both Spanish and English.

**2 guest rooms, 1 bath shared
by all
Budget
Smoking in limited areas only**

STARFISH

*F*or a truly memorable experience, make arrangements to stay at the brand-new Starfish, hosted by an Englishman and a Texan. This vivacious couple have fused two cultures into the unique blend that expresses itself in the home's decor.

The contemporary exterior of the Starfish, found in one of the city's newest subdivisions, is somewhat in contrast to the interior, which is a mixture of the Old World and the New. The colors of apricot, melon, peach, and white add vitality and brightness to the dark wooden English furniture, displaying the ability of this animated hostess to decorate. Plants abound, adding a kind of spontaneity that reflects the lifestyle of these very alive people.

Though guests are free to use all of the house, you'll wind up in the homey television room. Peach-printed slipcovers, made by the hostess's own hands, dress overstuffed chairs. Antique collectibles and greenery are in every corner, bringing the outside in. This sunny room opens onto a kitchen, the center of which is an old Victorian chopping block. Be sure to spend some time on the screened porch, which is covered with bougainvillea, moss roses, geraniums, and grapevines, and take the time to smell the roses. A bright red feeder beckons the hummingbird, while goldfish swim lazily in a little backyard pool.

At bedtime, you can choose one of the three upstairs guest rooms, with one that doubles as a guest sitting area for watching television or playing cards at the game table. The bath, also upstairs, is shared only by guests. Note that some of the artworks, as well as the bedspread and matching bed hanging, were created by the hostess.

You'll put off going to bed just to hear your host and hostess tell the endless stories connected with each piece of art and each antique. He is a British pilot in the process of becoming an American one. She is a Texas-born redhead who teaches the centuries-old skill of bobbinlace. They have no children but own two Chinese pugs, E. T. and R. P. (short for Roly Poly), and Chloe and Ember, two griffons, which are carriage dogs from Brussels bred hundreds of years ago to kill rats.

So if you don't mind the dogs, stay at the Starfish. You'll come away with much more than you bargained for.

3 guest rooms, 1 bath (shared)
Moderate
No children

Galveston
and Bacliff

BED AND BREAKFAST–
GALVESTON

Bed and Breakfast–Galveston, one of the newest and most organized B&B associations in Texas, will book your place on a passage back in time. Of the seven B&B listings here, all are historic, and each tells its own story of those Galvestonians who made their mark on history. You'll have your choice of gorgeous residences, Victorian homes that date back before the turn of the century, the elegant 1916 Guldmann Mansion, or a romantic high-raised cottage. Each one speaks for itself, with the graceful elegance of the past apparent in every nook and cranny. And you'll be greeted with that ageless southern hospitality that will make you consider Galveston a permanent home.

Though these B&Bs are some of the state's oldest structures, the association itself, which has been a long time coming, is one of the newest. Before its approval by city fathers, which came ironically on the day that Hurricane Alicia hit in 1983, the association was plagued by objections from ill-informed residents and officials. Heated debates lasted through two mayors and two different city councils, and the organization almost died on the vine and left prospective hosts and hostesses shaking their heads in dismay.

Pat Hanemann, however, cohost of the Gilded Thistle and the group's spearhead, would not give up. Time after time, he put his analytical mind to work, using his ability on every occasion to persuade those with influence that Galveston needed bed and breakfast. Finally, after miles of red tape regarding zoning, fire regulations, and health codes, Galveston's association became a reality. Today, Galveston leaders are content with an ordinance and fully support Pat and his B&B association.

As for Pat, he always knew the B&B concept would work. He was inspired by the stories that his mother, Helen, told of her travels as a child. She would set out from Austin with her grandparents for Ohio and Pennsylvania, where they would stay in "tourist homes." With this in mind, Pat convinced Helen to purchase a historic Victorian home in Galveston. Together they restored it, and today the Gilded Thistle stands as one of the best guest residences Texas has to offer.

As for the city, Galveston will spark interest in even the most blasé tourist. If your idea of a vacation is rest and relaxation, then spend all the time you like on the beach that stretches some thirty-two lazy miles. If you're sports-minded and want to catch the really big ones, you can deep-sea fish, seine, gig, fish in fresh water or surf, and crab. And of course, the gulf waters are warm and inviting, so bring your swimsuit.

Most everyone will want to visit the historic Strand, the Victorian "Wall Street of the Southwest." The old buildings, lit by gas streetlights, have been restored and now house shops, restaurants, and art galleries. The Strand also provides a wonderful setting for the Galveston Historical Foundation's "Dickens on the Strand," which takes place the first weekend in December. Experience an old-fashioned Christmas with this authentic Victorian holiday street scene. Thanks to developer George Mitchell and his wife, Cynthia, the Strand transforms at Mardi Gras time. To commemorate the opening of their historic Tremont Hotel in the early spring of 1985, George and Cynthia decided to revive the city's Mardi Gras celebration, which was held every year between 1867 and 1940. The event, once second only to the New Orleans festivities, now brings thousands to the island to view a spectacular parade, attend the grand ball and countless parties, and, of course, eat the best seafood on the coast. Be sure, however, to make reservations early.

If you find yourself hopelessly enchanted with the Strand, you'll love the Historic Homes Tour, which takes place annually on the second weekend in May. But don't fret if May is not convenient, because you can organize your own riding and walking tour of the East End Historical District, a forty-block area that is listed on the National Register of Historic Places. Go by the Historical Society's office on the Strand or write to the Chamber of Commerce for a guide brochure. Along this tour you'll see the famed Bishop's Palace, the John Clement Trube House ("the strangest house in a city of strange houses"), and the 1893 Baily-Phillips home, now the Gilded Thistle, among others.

If trains are more up your track, visit the Railroad Museum, which highlights forty railway cars. Don't miss the "people's gallery" at the Center for Transportation and Commerce, which is a dramatic plastered study of thirty-nine life-sized travelers immortally captured from a moment in Galveston's past. The setting is the Santa Fe Railroad Depot on a lazy afternoon in 1932. The still-life figures, frozen in place yet alive somehow, tell their own stories of life on the Gulf Coast.

If you plan to visit in the spring, go on the first or second Sunday after Easter for the Blessing of the Shrimp Fleet, an annual event where decorated shrimp trawlers compete for pageant honors and receive clergy blessings for a safe and productive harvest. Tour also the beautifully restored *Elissa*, an 1877 square-rigged merchant sailing ship. You'll find it on Pier 21. If salt suns deep in your veins, take the short trip by Bolivar Peninsula. You'll get a fish-eye view of Galveston Harbor and Seawolf Park.

Whatever you do, give yourself time to soak up the sun, surf, and scenery that are historic Galveston. The city tells its own story of Texas. So grab a train or jump in your car and head for the seawall. Who knows? You may decide to write yourself into Galveston's own colorful history.

Pat Hanemann, director
1805 Broadway
Galveston 77550
(409) 762-0854

GILDED THISTLE

*I*f phrases like "treetop nursery" and "stairway to nowhere" tickle your curiosity, or if you've always wanted to know more about the Texas Rangers than the history books would tell you, then the Gilded Thistle on Galveston Island is for you. Built in 1893 and known historically as the Baily-Phillips home, owner Helen Hanemann and her son Pat named it after the very hearty plant that, in Pat's words, "propagates itself selectively along Gulf Coast seashores, almost as if it had chosen that spot." He goes on to explain that the "thistle has waged a war against time, and though it produces prickly leaves, it also yields a beautiful blossom." The Gilded Thistle is thus apropos not only of the house, which has withstood more than ninety years of history, but also of the island and its people, who have endured all kinds of adversity. It was this endurance that resulted in Galveston's flowering into a "gilded age" of prosperity.

The story of this old survivor began with John E. Baily, general manager and secretary-treasurer of the bustling port, who built the structure as a part-time residence in 1893. Then in 1908 the home was purchased by an Englishman, William Parr of the successful William Parr Shipping Company, the oldest of its kind still in existence. Parr's company handled the shipping of commodities such as imported Portland cement (the same substance with which the seawall was built), Belgian brick, and Liverpool salt. It exported cotton and other raw materials to English textile mills. Parr left his company and his house to his nephew, Ben Phillips, who successfully continued in his uncle's footsteps. In fact, Ben's sons still own the company today. An accomplished cellist, Ben organized a chamber music ensemble, which played for many of the prominent citizens of the day and also for Gilbert and Sullivan at the opera house in 1894. On very frequent occasions, the ensemble played to small groups in the parlor of the Baily-Phillips home.

But life in the historic dwelling was not always music and happiness. An extortion plot caused Ben's wife Katherine, known lovingly as Key, to have part of the back stairs removed to discourage criminals from entering the home from the rear. The "stairway to nowhere" is still present as a reminder of the dark cloud that once hung over the contented family. Helen is quick to tell you that Key, who has not been among the living for some time, still resides in the house. This benevolent ghost disagrees with the placement of pictures in the kitchen and has on occasion taken the liberty of moving them.

Key certainly doesn't have much to complain about in regard to the way Helen and Pat have chosen to restore and decorate the Gilded Thistle. Inside and out, the charming Queen Anne structure, with its wraparound porch, reflects the *joie de vivre* evident in the past and present residing families. Spacious rooms decorated in fine period antiques and graceful screened porches filled with bromeliads, giant schefflera, and blooming hibiscus create an atmosphere of warmth and hominess. Potpourri wreaths and dried flower arrangements, Helen's own creations, appeal to the senses in such a way that memories of a nostalgic past immediately surface. Helen has also added needlepoint touches throughout the home, as well as her extensive collection of sea shells, which reveal her passionate love for the sea. This admiration for the water had apparently been shared by Baily, who chose ornamental tilework around the fireplaces that display the sea motif. In the foyer, for instance, fireplace tiles combine to create a picture of two women at the seaside. In the master bedroom, the seafarer's rope loops around the inviting hearth. Pat's blood, sweat, and tears went into the restoration, and he suggests that to experience this B&B at its best, you should come during the spring or fall when large walk-through windows and transoms are opened to let in the cooling sea breezes. Once you've sat on the back porch and indulged yourself in a cup of steaming brew and had Helen's hearty continental treats, you'll beg this hostess to adopt you. If you find the soft sea winds so intoxicating that you can't keep your eyes open, return to your upstairs room and go to bed.

There are three guest rooms in all; the master bedroom has a fireplace and private bath. Ask Helen and Pat about the picture of their ancestor, Captain Dan Roberts, founder of the Carlsbad Caverns enterprise and a noted Texas Ranger. The "boys' room," decorated by Pat with an Oriental motif, has its own screened porch. He has used ginger and cinnabar with Oriental umbrellas to create a scene that a romance writer would love. Be sure to notice the framed piece of lace from Helen's great-great-grandmother's wedding gown. The "treetop nursery" is shaded by trees, thus the name. Decorated in blues and gold, the room houses a turn-of-the-century bureau, as well as an old Pullman chair and an antique alarm clock. A bath is shared by guests of the "boys' room" and the nursery.

If you listen closely enough, you might hear Ben playing his cello over the sea breezes as they brush the branches up against the house. Or you may even see Key in her Red Cross uniform rearranging the pictures in the kitchen. But one thing is for certain: you'll be safe and comfortable here. In fact, you'll feel that you've finally come home.

1805 Broadway
Galveston 77550
(409) 763-0194
3 guest rooms, 1 private bath,
1 shared bath
Exclusive
Smoking in limited areas
No children. No pets.

HAZLEWOOD HOUSE

*L*ocated on Galveston's historic East End, the romantic Hazlewood House stands only six blocks from the surf yet only twelve blocks from the Strand. This charmingly ornate Victorian raised cottage is overseen by the equally charming Pat Hazlewood, a "venture capitalist" (as she calls herself), who dabbles in Galveston real estate and restoration consultation. Versed in the art of southern hospitality, Pat will make you feel at home here in this cozy abode built in 1877 by the young lawyer Charles Cleveland as a wedding present for his bride. As their marriage did, the house withstood the test of time, for it was built of sturdy cypress brought to the island on sailing ships from Maine.

This yellow- and green-shuttered B&B, situated on a shady corner of Church, is simply alive with atmosphere. It is raised a good five feet off the ground, leaving a space that for years was used as a wash area for servants. Porches characterize the entire front and sides of the cottage, creating a perfect setting. As you enter the front door, which is actually on the east side of the house, you'll walk into the formal Victorian-furnished dining room,

Gilded Thistle

where Pat's scrumptious breakfast is served. All the white-plastered walls and rich wood wainscoting are beautifully preserved and add a dramatic color contrast to the traditional dark-paneled walls. Transoms, too, permit sunlight to flow into the cottage, giving a light, airy effect. Curtained French doors separate the first guest room, which opens onto the porch, from the dining area. Be sure to spend an hour or two one evening whiling away some time on the candlelit porch, which also has a small romantic fountain. The second largest bedroom is the most sensuous, with a king-sized bed dressed in lace and linen finery, a richly planked wood ceiling, and subdued lighting. The small bronze sculpture that stands on the antique dresser is of Pat herself. It was created by a former husband. Of the bronze, which is reminiscent of Art Nouveau, Pat openly teases, "I've been married four times—three doctors and one sculptor, and the sculptor was the best." Also noteworthy in this room is the old wooden stove, which kept many a body warm in its day, and an old sundial, topped with glass and used for an end table. The third guest room is at the back of the house and is decorated in Indian motif, the American Indian being a subject of particular interest to Pat. The crocheted bedspread was made by her grandmother.

Two baths serve the three guest rooms, and one is equipped with a soothing Jacuzzi. The second bathroom, reminiscent of a throne room, has an old-fashioned wooden potty with carved armrests mounted and outfitted with totally modern plumbing. It's perfect for the man who would be king. Across from the throne is an antique mirrored hall tree that creatively houses a sink.

But for the ultimate in atmosphere, sit awhile on the west porch and enjoy your complimentary glass of wine, along with fruit and cheese. Pat also serves complimentary hot chocolate, cider, or toddy if you want it. Tea and fresh-baked cookies can be served inside or out on the west porch. There's a wonderful hammock out there—a perfect spot in which to soak up a little local color. Your wish is Pat's command, but be sure to take the time to get to know her. She knows much about Galveston, especially the historic sector.

Though Pat purchased Hazlewood House in 1977 from Nellie Sullivan, its resident since 1912, she feels that she has always belonged here. "The people who lived here were happy and content. As a result, I feel safe here," she says. And it's obvious that she, too, is happy and content, ready to share her feeling of goodwill with you.

1127 Church
Galveston 77550
(409) 762-1668

3 guest rooms (one with Jacuzzi)
1 private and 1 shared bath
Exclusive
No children. No pets.

MATALÍ

*T*he Matalí, a true example of East-
lake Victorian design, has now joined the growing number of historic B&Bs
on Galveston Island. Featured on the 1984 Historical Homes Tour, the structure, built by the successful ship chandler Samuel Maas for his family, became a monument to the love that existed between him and the Cologne-born
Isabella Offenbach. Though records indicate that construction (or reconstruction) occurred in 1886, it is assumed that the original home, built
around 1844, was either totally destroyed or sustained heavy damage during
the devastating fire of November 13, 1885, which claimed a forty-block section of Galveston.

At any rate, the Samuel Maas family roots begin here. Samuel fell in love
with the striking songbird Isabella while she sang in the cathedral of Cologne. A daughter of the rabbi of Cologne and the sister of the famous com-
poser Offenbach, Isabella consented to marry him and return to Galveston to
make a new home. To Samuel's delight, his bride charmed everyone she met,
endearing her to the people of the island. A member of the Lutheran church,
she became a pillar of respectability by also establishing the German Ladies
Benevolent Society in 1874. When Isabella died in 1891, the home was sold
to Dr. W. C. Fisher, who in 1928 sold it to Amadeo Matalí. Amadeo, too,
existed happily in the home with his wife. In fact, testimony to their love can
be found on the original front-yard bench and birdbath. He personally com-
missioned the pieces for Mrs. Matalí and placed the inscription on each.
They read simply, "Neni," Amadeo's nickname for his wife.

Maas finished the home itself as one would a painting or sculpture. Eastlake trim, rosetted ceilings, and beautiful stained-glass windows all pulsate

the happiness that once existed here. Above exterior side windows, for example, are handsome designs of the rising and setting sun. The jeweled stained-glass pieces, particularly the religious one above the fireplace in the parlor, reflect Isabella's love of her church. Ornate archways, large bay windows, and eleven-foot cypress doors let plenty of light and breezes into this bluish-grey-and-white-trimmed B&B. You'll also see a variety of woods, from cherry and mahogany mantelpieces to wainscoting of curly pine.

Today, the Matalí is owned by accountant Dan Dyer, who has taken pains to restore the home to its original beauty, even down to the porcelain doorknobs and pine floors. As a guest, you will have your choice of one of three tastefully decorated centrally air-conditioned and heated rooms with their own porches. There are two bathrooms upstairs for guest use.

Dan provides guests with an evening cheese tray and a hearty continental breakfast. At the front door you can board the Galveston trolley, which will take you to the historic Strand. If you wait long enough, you'll see a Galveston touring horse and buggy pass by. In fact, for a Victorian view of the East End, flag down a coachman and climb aboard. It will be a ride worth remembering.

1727 Sealy
Galveston 77550
(409) 763-4526
3 guest rooms
1 shared and 1 private bath
Exclusive
No children under 12. No pets.

MATHER-ROOT HOUSE

*A*s our history books have repeatedly told us, Americans continue to flock to major cities in search of a better way of life. The drawing card is the bigger buck, with promises of a more affluent future. But for many, the price they have had to pay has been too high, with big-city pressures chipping away at leisure time and peace of mind. So along with the influx of big-city newcomers has been the silent exiting of professionals in search of a quieter life.

For one such couple, Ben and Linda Price, Galveston Island is that life. They longed for a more peaceful home life but didn't want to give up their Houston jobs. (Linda is administrator of the Harris County Psychiatric Hospital in Houston, and Ben is manager of western gas acquisition for the American Natural Resources Company.) Having already restored two old homes in the Houston Heights area, they were determined to find a residence steeped in history and nostalgia, yet one that would lend itself to the B&B idea. They settled on the historic Mather-Root home, and construction began. By Christmas 1984, another Galveston bed and breakfast was born.

And what a B&B it is, a Victorian structure that was on the city's annual historic tour in 1976 and encompassing some 10,000 square feet. Every foot is elegant, from a unique loft that seconds as the owners' private suite, to the authentic butler's pantry, to the carriage house. The best part about this blue and white Victorian, however, is that the Prices are willing to share their home with B&B guests.

Records have not yielded definite proof about the Mather-Root home's beginnings. It is known that the house was built somewhere between 1898 and 1903. The builder is thought to have been C. F. W. Felt, chief civil engineer to the Gulf, Colorado and Santa Fe Railway Company, and that he probably sold it to Mrs. M. S. Mather around 1896, who then sold it to Cornelia P. Root in 1903. Records indicate that Mrs. Root, a widow, spent a fortune either repairing or rebuilding the home. Speculation has it that the residence was a victim of the 1903 storm. Dr. Marvin Graves, a prominent physician at the University of Texas Medical School, later bought it, becoming its third owner. Today, the Prices occupy the lovely two-and-a-half-story frame home, which is an attempt to reconcile Greek Revival with the Victorian style.

The interesting architectural combination of the Greek with the turn-of-the-century influence can be seen in the flowing semicircular porch, its neoclassical columns, and the scroll effect on interior archways. The imposing entrance hall, with its authentic antique Art Nouveau electric and gas light fixtures, features a carved burled wood staircase and two stained-glass windows in pastel shades with buttons of red jewel glass. The balusters are turned, and ribbon and bellflower carvings are carried through on the upper landing newel and the head of the stairs.

Galveston, ahead of its time at the turn of the century, was one of the first cities to get electric lighting. Considered one of the new "modern houses," the Mather-Root residence was one of the first to have combination gas and electric lights. But of particular interest are the hexagonal-shaped rooms, which provide for better circulation. The only square room in the house is the kitchen.

In keeping with the home's history, Linda has chosen period wallpapers and lively colored fabrics to decorate this B&B, including the three air-conditioned guest rooms. The Wicker Room, which is available for guest use, opens on the back balcony, which overlooks the newly added pool. The shared bath, with original sink and cut-glass fixtures, separates the Wicker Room from a peach-colored guest room, which has its own lavatory. But the most impressive room is the elegant Champagne Suite, with a sitting area that opens to the front balcony. Champagne is the order of the day for guests who stay here.

Located on the historic East End, this B&B is five blocks from the Strand and a carriage ride away from Stewart Beach, the Bishop's Palace, and the University of Texas Medical Branch.

1816 Winnie
Galveston 77550
(409) 765-7335
3 guest rooms
1 private and 1 shared bath
Exclusive
No children under 12. No pets.
Carriage house apartment also
available

Mather-Root House

MICHAEL'S—HANS GULDMANN MANSION

*H*ans Guldmann, Galveston's onetime vice-consul for Denmark and a prominent director of the South Texas Cotton Oil Company, was a perfectionist in search of the finer things in life. But where most spent a lifetime seeking but never finding, Hans, master of a virtual fleet of yachts, had it all and didn't mind paying the price. In fact, Hans and his wife were the epitomes of that golden era when America was chugging full-steam ahead into the fast and furious 1920s. Together they made their 5,000-square-foot home a showplace that was the setting for many of Galveston's most elaborate affairs.

Today, however, the Hans Guldmann mansion is one of the city's newest and biggest B&Bs, brought back to life by Houston lawyer Allen Isbell and his wife, Mikey. They were intrigued by the home's history and with Hans, a man who was determined to make the mansion a veritable fortress.

The story of this beautiful residence began in 1915, the year of a devastating storm. Guldmann began construction that apparently suffered heavy damage as a result of hurricane winds and rising tides. Displeased with workmanship that couldn't withstand Galveston storms, he had the existing three-story structure torn down and begun again. This time he instructed that the concrete bags that had been soaked during the hurricane be packed in the foundation and the front sloping terrace to prevent subsidence. He also ordered thick, sturdy glass (still present) in all the windows and doors to sustain tidal gusts. For sunny, breezy days, he ordered verandas, sun porches, swivel-glass windows, and transoms in profusion. The grounds were transformed into elaborate gardens, with pergolas, tennis courts, and grape vineyards, providing the Guldmanns with adequate space to accommodate the large numbers of foreign dignitaries and guests who attended their frequent parties and receptions. Those lucky enough to be invited could sit around the lovely fountain (which is still there) and the concrete pond filed with goldfish, or stroll into Mrs. Guldmann's greenhouse to view her prize ferns, begonias, and roses. She especially loved roses and once had pergolas covered with every color and variety imaginable. Guests could also entertain themselves by watching pet doves as they cooled themselves in their large concrete birdbath (also still there), built in the bird sanctuary.

Michael's—Hans Guldmann Mansion

Though the grounds were of most interest to Mrs. Guldmann, the imposing red concrete structure was Hans's pride and joy. He made the numerous rooms large and open, with a dining room big enough to accommodate the family table that seated twenty. The room opened onto the massive living room, making it ample for the annual Cotton Seed Crushers convention. Records have revealed that Mrs. Guldmann was an experienced hostess who on one occasion decorated the entire yard with Japanese lanterns and hired a full orchestra to provide the music. Hans built a shooting gallery in the giant cellar, which also housed the family vat for making wine. Ask to see the wine cellar, which is also below. Remnants of the Guldmann stock remain.

The Guldmanns have long since vanished from 1715 35th St., but the home and its remaining one acre have been restored and opened by Allen and Mikey. Three rooms with shared baths are available upstairs. The furnishings are eclectic, with family antiques combined with a more contemporary look. The house is also full of art and sculpture, some done by local artists. If you stay here, ask Mikey to show you the nine-spigot shower in the master bath.

Have an evening cup of coffee and some of Mikey's heavenly cheesecake with your host and hostess on one of the verandas. And perhaps, if you imagine hard enough, you might find yourself transported back into the 1920s, where you are the honored guest of Hans Guldmann and a willing participant at the annual Cotton Seed Crushers ball.

1715 35th
Galveston 77550
(409) 763-3760
3 guest rooms, 2 shared baths
Exclusive
No pets
Hearty continental breakfast
provided

J. F. SMITH HOUSE

*R*obert Clark, owner of Brad-
shaw's Flower Shop, and Galveston developer William S. Cherry, in connection with the J. F. Smith House Limited Partners, are credited with opening
this historic bed and breakfast, having purchased the beautiful Italianate former residence of J. F. Smith in 1984. Smith, a past owner of J. F. Smith and
Brothers Hardware Store, would be proud to see his home standing regally on
Broadway Blvd., fully restored to its original 1885 state.

The house itself is a study in architecture and would interest even the most
blasé visitor, with its Eastlake stickstyle mantels, original gold-leaf molding,
and massive twelve-foot doors, dwarfed by sixteen-foot ceilings. Cherry and
mahogany fireplaces are found in just about every room, a necessary characteristic common to most old houses in order to bring warmth to otherwise
drafty, chilly parlors and bedrooms. Happily, Robert and Bill are among the
electric company's most respected customers, as modern heat and air-
conditioning will make your stay with them much more pleasurable. But even
if the air-conditioning didn't exist, large transoms and ceiling fans would
keep even a Texas greenhorn cool.

It would even be worth a little sweat just to see all the elegant touches,
such as the encaustic tile entry, interestingly found between two sets of
double front doors, or the striking Eastlake stairway with its carved mahogany and walnut banister. Also noteworthy are the *faux bois* finish of the
pocket doors, the gracefully arched windows, and the old linoleum rug in the
back hall that great-grandmother would have given her best ivory brooch to
have. While you're standing there admiring the rug, look up and study the
fascinating stained-glass window. This one and the other in the dining room
are virtual studies in the Victorian technique of glass cutting.

While you're gazing skyward, admire the pressed tin ceiling and ornate
Victorian chandelier in the back parlor. Most of the original gas lights are
extant, and believe it or not, the hundred-year-old skeleton keys can still be
found in the brass locks under the original porcelain knobs!

If you don't wish to stay in one of the two guest rooms with a bath, then make arrangements to stay in the beautifully restored carriage house out back. The accommodations are comfortable, with a lovely view from the terrace of the spider lilies and daylilies, ginger, and pyracanthas that dot the garden. The focal point of the greenery is the half-century-old magnolia that hovers over the garden like a southern nanny guarding her children.

2217 Broadway
Galveston 75550
(409) 765-5121
6 guest rooms, each with bath
Exclusive
No children under 12. No pets.
Smoking in limited areas
Carriage house available

VICTORIAN INN

*I*t's a sunny morning at Galveston's Victorian Inn, and you're sitting on the front porch swing having coffee. The air smells fresh and clean, with only traces of the smell of the fresh paint that covers the eighty-year-old home. If you listen carefully, you can hear the Gulf bringing in its morning tide over the quiet clatter of your hostess, who is in the kitchen making a second pot of coffee. You are perfectly relaxed, and at that very moment your only concern is keeping your hot coffee shielded from the cooling coastal breezes. And then it hits you—the aroma of home-made banana nut bread and scrumptious breakfast rolls just out of the oven—and you suddenly realize that you're famished. It soon becomes obvious that you have found paradise.

Even Grandma would have felt at home at the Victorian Inn. A survivor of the Great Storm of 1900 that literally flattened the island, killing six thousand residents, the red and white wood three-story structure has withstood the Great Depression, two world wars, and the many hurricanes that have plagued the twentieth century. Built in 1899 by cement contractor Isaac Hefron, the home, now on the National Register of Historic Places, stands as a beautiful reminder of workmanship that is gone with an age. Hefron spared no expense, with Belgian tiled fireplaces and private wraparound balconies in every centrally cooled and heated bedroom, and the huge walk-through windows to ensure the cooling circulation of the sea breezes. Hefron also acquired the best artisans in the city to lay hardwood pegged floors, carve intricate scrollwork on staircases and on a curious little nook once used by the Hefron children as a place to study or play cards. The spacious second floor is made up of four large bedrooms, with three named after the Hefron children and the fourth after Isaac. There is a small room off Amy's Room with space enough for just its single bed that would be perfect for a couple with an older child. (The management asks that children be at least twelve years old.) The third floor is also being made into guest quarters; the managers reside on the first floor. As for the decor, owner Don Mafridge has put much money and effort into this showplace, which has been featured on the Galveston Historical Foundation's Tour of Homes. Mr. Mafridge has purchased period antiques that complement the Victorian elegance of the inn and has chosen light, cheery fabric draperies and bedspreads to give it a homey, graceful mood.

For a taste of what is was like to live in Galveston at the turn of the century, stay at the wonderful Victorian Inn on the corner of 17th and Post Office. But plan your schedule with a few days to spare. because once you get there, you'll want to stay and stay and stay.

511 17th
Galveston 77550
(409) 762-3235
4 guest rooms
2 shared baths, 1 private bath
Exclusive
No children under 12. No pets.

SMALL INN

*S*tand at this B&B's front door and drink in a view of Galveston Bay that is so spectacular that it would make even Captain Ahab's eyes water. Sailboats paint triangles on the horizon, while shrimpers chug home with their catches of the day. A colony of pelicans and a couple of gulls sit on a distant dock, watching for an unsuspecting mullet jumping in the waves. You have a choice of either casting your line out off the private dock or lying under the sun next to the romantic cloverleaf pool, which divides the luxury home from the bluff that stops at the sea.

Whatever your wish is this host and hostess's command. They have renovated their home to give the maximum view of the water by glassing the entire front. The large living and dining area combines with the kitchen to make a large sunny sitting area where you can contemplate the view. A full breakfast is also served at this choice spot. The hostess serves a variety of delights, from Eggs Benedict to omelets and from biscuits to homemade zucchini bread. Sausage or bacon is always served, as well as fresh fruit, coffee, or tea.

You can bet your best fishing lure that the food will please even the most discriminating epicurean, because the hostess is in the catering business. Socially and culturally minded, she is also a dominating force among Bay-area symphony leaguers and helps to bring high-quality music to the area. She is also active in the local attempt to incorporate Bacliff, Bayview, and San Leon. Your host, a soft-spoken man who dabbles in real estate investments, has been a chemical engineer with Monsanto for a number of years. He enjoys boating, shrimping, and water skiing and can give you such particulars as where to launch your boat. The well-traveled couple have stayed in B&Bs from Australia to New Zealand to New York City.

The guest room, with a private bath, is secluded but very accessible to the family room and kitchen. The hostess chose the Oriental motif on which to base the room's decor with a Japanese and a Korean kimono mounted as wall hangings. The Japanese piece was brought back from overseas by the hostess's father during World War II. Delicate Oriental fans and crossed obis are also mounted, carrying through the room's theme. The spread on the king-sized bed picks up the colors of the hangings, giving a light, cheery mood that is characteristic of the entire home. Guests are provided with a television and an extra cot if it is needed.

When you pull into the driveway of this seaside retreat, don't be alarmed
by the family collie and the giant St. Bernard. They're harmless and see
themselves as the official greeters. Once you get settled, be sure to have a
seafood lunch or dinner on the coast. On Nasa Road 1, Louie's on the Lake in
Seabrook specializes in a different seafood every night. It's buffet style and a
little expensive, but worth it. In Kemah, try the Flying Dutchman or Pier 8,
and to soak up a little local color, try Clifton by the Sea in Bacliff. It's right
on the water and has been an area landmark since 1905. If you would rather
play bingo than eat, you're in the right place. Games are played every afternoon and evening in the area. For the local nightspots, ask your host and
hostess. They like to dance, and they know the good ones.

4815 W. Bayshore
Bacliff 77518
(713) 339-3489
1 guest room, 1 private bath
Moderate
No restrictions
Note to those in wheelchairs:
This B&B is barrier-free.

Goliad

WHITE HOUSE INN

*I*n February 1836, Colonel James Walker Fannin, a West Point dropout and a pillar of indecision, passed up his chance to be a Texas hero. While camped at Goliad with 400 men, William B. Travis sent four pleas to Fannin to come and render aid to his company of 188 defenders, who were fighting desperately at the Alamo. Travis and his followers, among them such legends as Davy Crockett and Jim Bowie, succeeded in holding off Santa Anna's 2,400 Mexicans until March 6, when the mission was stormed and all defenders of the Alamo lay dead. Fannin paid for his sin against Texas, however; he and his men were taken by General Urrea, who was ordered by Santa Anna to shoot the prisoners. The bodies were burned, then tossed into a common grave.

Today Goliad is literally alive with Texas history. Go there and you can travel back to the Spanish mission days at Presidio de la Bahía, remember the fight for Texas independence at Fannin State Park, or relive the stormy days of the Cart War of 1857. (This squabble between Mexican and Texas teamsters resulted in bodies dangling from the Hanging Tree on Goliad's square.)

With all of its history, it is no wonder that Goliad appealed to Ruby Mennich as the perfect place for a bed and breakfast. This sturdy old home was built in 1935 by the widow of W. O. Huggins, a Texas lawyer of note and editor of the *Houston Chronicle*. The old steam radiators still clank out a cozy heat on chilly days.

The White House Inn offers three charming guest rooms, each with its own bath. While the furnishings are not antiques, they are homey and comfortable. A favorite of the three is the one Ruby has converted from the old servants' quarters downstairs and off the main house. This lovely retreat offers a maximum of privacy.

Ruby is well known around Goliad for her fabulous cooking, and her catering is always in demand. The Inn's dining-room table often groans with good food for special parties. For her guests, Ruby serves a memorable breakfast, which is included in the price of the room. Whether you want a hearty meal to start your day, or just to nibble on a piece of dry toast, you are seated in the dining room with crisp white linens and silver serving pieces. The full breakfast menu varies, but it is always substantial and includes such goodies as homemade jams and jellies. What a great way to break a fast! Ruby also leaves a dish of homemade brownies or cookies in each room in case you want an extra snack.

Innkeepers Jan and Mert Rawson are always on hand to make you feel welcome, and Jan keeps the kitchen filled with the aroma of something delicious baking in the oven. Stop in Goliad for a spell. You'll learn a little Texas history while being pampered at your own personal White House.

P. O. Box 637, 203 N.
Commercial
Goliad 77963
(512) 645-2701
3 guest rooms, each with
private bath
Moderate
No pets

Houston (Includes Alvin and Bryan)

BED AND BREAKFAST SOCIETY OF HOUSTON

*I*n 1982 Debbie Siegel, the founder of Houston's B&B association, saw a need to preserve the fading small-town atmosphere of Houston, then one of the fastest-growing boomtowns in the country. She looked around and saw slick glassed hotels popping up everywhere and wondered if the B&B idea would take root and grow among the space-age structures. Having traveled the bed and breakfast circuit in Europe and in northern California, Debbie went to her mentor, Kenn Knopp, who heads the very successful Fredericksburg Bed and Breakfast. Kenn gave her advice and encouragement, and armed with determination, Debbie returned to Houston to set the idea in motion. Then Marguerite Swanson, an antiques collector and one skilled in the art of hospitality, soon joined her; before they knew it, the Houston B&B association had grown to include under its umbrella a variety of listings. Today Marguerite is the sole owner of this association, which serves virtually every area of Houston. Obviously the B&B idea did take root in Space City, U.S.A. You can now stay in a homey, personalized environment while enjoying one of the most versatile cities in the world. Go out and explore the city of many faces, but stay at a Houston guest home. Your host will be able to give you some great tips on things to do and see.

Houston itself has come a long way since real estate promoters August and John Allen set foot on the mosquito-infested site in 1836. The brothers made their way through the tangled undergrowth and in spite of the stifling heat saw a place of financial promise. To these foresighted individuals, the 6,642 acres they bought near the headwaters of Buffalo Bayou would become the promised land.

And promises it kept, not only for the Allens but also for the millions who have come after them. Rich soil has produced high agricultural yields, especially in the timber industry. Houston was once compared to a farmer reaping from the land wealth enough for the body and soul. But at the beginning of the twentieth century, the image of Houston as a tall Texas farmer with a dirt-soiled face changed to that of an oilfield worker drenched in black gold. The striking of oil at Spindletop in 1901 forced the city into a whole new era. Rigs began to dot Texas farmlands and prairies, and as time passed, Houston began to pump the profits. As a result, Houston is today the home base for most of the nation's major oil and offshore companies.

Oilmen were not the only ones to come to the promised land. The Texas Medical Center began to draw some of the biggest names in medicine, and of course Houston's reputation for high-quality health care grew. The city was given another whole new dimension, with physicians and researchers integrating into the population. If this weren't enough, the area's economy was given yet another shot in the arm when NASA moved in, bringing with it scientists, astronauts, and technologists. Artists, architects, and artisans followed, hungry for the taste of the good life and hearing the call of a virgin city destined for greatness. Intellectuals and cowpokes alike began to call Houston home, creating an intriguing blend that can only be found here. Now Houston has it all, from professional opportunities to arts and amusements to the best medical care in the world. So, partner, head your horse toward the big city, but go with one word of caution: steer your steed away from the freeways during rush hours!

Marguerite Swanson, director
9726 Truscon
Houston 77080
(713) 468-6220

NO. 1

*F*or the bed and breakfast guest who would like to experience the true lap of luxury, posh accommodations can be found in the heart of Houston's Memorial area. Every inch of this beautifully decorated patio home reflects the artistic flair of its owner. As is customary with patio homes, the entire thirteen-year-old residence is surrounded by gardens, with the actual square structure built around a lush green garden patio. Blooming bromeliads, ferns, elephant ears, and varieties of tropical foliage make breakfast dining comparable to eating in a veritable Garden of Eden. When weather permits, the hostess serves her delicacies on the patio, which is furnished with white wrought-iron furniture. However, even on rainy, cold days, guests only have to gaze from any room onto the home's glassed gallery to enjoy nature, with the breakfast nook providing clear views not only of the terrace but also of the exterior ivy-covered landscape, complete with a rustic birdhouse.

Guests are also taken with the exquisite furnishings that are so characteristic of their owner. The focal point of the contemporary living area is a black baby grand piano. Indian and Eskimo artifacts, weavings, and an antique tool collection decorate the bookshelves and walls, providing much food for thought and conversation. One of the most impressive pieces lies at the feet of the admiring visitor. An Edward Fields handwoven contemporary rug, designed by the owner's husband (whose field of study was the oil industry), symbolizes the different strata of the earth with its sculptured textures and earthy tones. This beautiful design acts as a centralizing element, unifying the room to make it truly a place of beauty. Virtually every room contains items that arouse interest. For example, the guest room, furnished with French Provincial furniture complemented by draperies and a spread of peach and gold, holds within an étagère a collection of antique Finnic trowels. There is a second room with hideaway beds that could be used to accommodate a larger party. The rooms, which open onto the gallery, are joined by a guest bath.

The hostess is representative of the successful businesswoman, and her grace and poise immediately set guests at ease. Not only does she provide her visitors with lively, intelligent conversation, but she also prepares an elegant breakfast, which frequently includes Eggs Benedict, croissants, English muffins, and fresh fruit.

For a romantic feel of Houston hospitality and ambience at its finest, stay at this alluring Memorial B&B. It is a private nature sanctuary in the middle of one of the world's busiest cities. Yet you only have to step outside its boundaries to encounter the excitement that is Houston.

2 guest rooms, 1 shared bath
Moderate
No children under 5. No pets.

NO. 2

*F*or Houstonians, the Montrose area has come into its own, as a haven for artists, restaurateurs, and even young executives who want to live closer to downtown. Filled with large old homes that were almost victims of urban decay, the Montrose area is now flourishing, its residents using its historic nature to advantage. Today, art galleries, European restaurants, and restored private residences characterize this arty uptown sector. If you want to be close to the city's very essence, where all the major attractions are only minutes away, stay at this intriguing bed and breakfast.

The late 1920s brown and white home is decorated to reflect the wide travels and experiences of its hostess. Eclectically furnished in a mixture of antiques with the traditional, the home sports shiny hardwood floors and wide, sunny windows. As you walk past the porch and through the front door, you'll find yourself in the spacious living room, which opens onto the dining room. The rooms are color coordinated in burgundy, cream, and mauve, with matching rugs that act as a unifying element. The furnishings range from a New Orleans pie safe to a wild cherry secretary made by a master craftsman from Campbellsville, Kentucky. Through her choice of decor, this hostess has succesfully blended the present with the past.

Also reminiscent of times past are the pretty guest bedroom and private bath at the top of the stairs. Totally remodeled, the room is always bathed in light because of six large windows covered with eggshell sheers that hang from brass rods. The light blue carpet adds warmth, while the orchid, purple, and white flowered wallpaper and bedspreads provide a touch of spring. The room is furnished with twin beds, a chest of drawers, a little table, and a white wicker chair. The Art Nouveau lamp belonged to the hostess's grandmother, adding a note of nostalgia to the room, which has its own air-conditioning and black-and-white television.

Art lovers will enjoy this lady's wide variety of art pieces, which come from all over the world. In the living room are seven little figurines that represent the Japanese gods of wealth, militarism, profit, longevity, wisdom, art and literature, and the patron saint of the fisherman and tradesman. Made by a Japanese woodcutter in Nara, they date from after World War II. Note also the collection next to them of New Orleans doubloons, all thrown from the Crewe of Rex floats during Mardi Gras and all in consecutive order beginning with 1960. This hostess, who once lived in the French Quarter, also has the 1976 Jazz Heritage Festival print, numbered and mounted, as well as several prints by Toulouse Lautrec, with two of her favorites being the poster of singer Aristide Bruant and the dancer Marcelle Lender. Also characteristic of New Orleans are two pieces in the dining room. One, a woodblock print by Zavier de Calletey called "Flambeau," represents the black Flambeau carrier that once preceded the Mardi Gras parades. The other is a pen-and-ink drawing of the famed French Market on Jackson Square.

The Louisiana influence is also alive and well in the manner in which breakfast is served. Though sometimes a continental breakfast of fresh fruit, hot muffins, and coffee or tea is determined by the schedule of the hostess, the morning fare may be quite different. This hostess has been known to serve such delights as cheese grits casserole, eggs and sausage soufflé, Pancake Oscar, and French omelets, for which the hostess prides herself in using the "no-hands" method, where she "shakes" the eggs.

So join this accomplished lady for her French omelets. Remember that she lives in exciting Montrose, where the chic have learned to live with the avant-garde, blending into a Houston breed unlike any other.

1 guest room with private bath
Moderate
No children. No pets.

NO. 3

*T*he affluent Braeswood area, a crape myrtle–lined subdivision near downtown Houston, provides a lovely setting for one of the city's most convenient B&Bs. It is the home of a couple whose wide range of interests varies from electric trains to an antique iron collection to an unusual display of encolay stone plates that depict poetry from the Romantic period. But most important, this host and hostess are definitely people-oriented and know the finer points of hospitality. It is they who have made their Old English–style house, nestled pleasantly among trees on a cul-de-sac, so inviting.

Guests have the privilege of privacy if they stay here, as the entire upstairs is devoted to as many as four guests at a time. There are two guest rooms, combined by a parlor furnished in antiques (there's a color television here) and a shared bath. One bedroom is decorated in yellows and is traditionally furnished in mahogany. The darkness of the matching bureau, dresser, and double bed is a pleasant contrast with the light fabrics and the comfortable white wicker rocker. The porcelain lamp, encolay stone plate, and 365-day

Houston Number 2

clock add a touch of yesteryear, and the period ceiling fans in both rooms not only contribute to the atmosphere but also add cooling to the centrally air-conditioned home.

The second, larger bedroom is in contrast with the first; the decor is traditionally modern, with white Italian-style furniture complemented by blue fabrics. Ask your host to show you the little cache that houses his electric train collection.

More trains are found in the living area, which has a fireplace and wet bar. The model cars are arranged among such conversation pieces as the fourth-generation mantel clock, made around 1876, which not only tells the time but also the day, the month, and the date. Note also the pleasantly inviting breakfast nook that opens onto the kitchen. The family's pet parrot will keep you company while you have coffee. Two thirty-gallon tanks full of freshwater fish add to the serene mood. Ask your host to tell you about the hand-dyed hooked rug in the entry, made by his ninety-year-old mother. The all-wool floral carpet was made from old wool garments that she collected and purchased. The effort that this artist put into the project is phenomenal, and the result is indeed a product of this lady's artistic abilities. While you're standing there, glance into the formal living and dining rooms. They are very pleasant, but you will probably want to eat your breakfast on the shaded backyard patio.

Caladiums, impatiens, and periwinkles accent the flagstones that outline the flower beds and oak trees. A birdbath and fountain under a shady elm constitute perfect surroundings not only for the B&B guest, but also for a variety of squirrels and birds. You are also welcome to use the hot tub.

As for the breakfast fare, it's as light as the European counterpart, but sufficient, with juice, fresh fruit, sweet rolls, or coffee cake. You can have cereal if you want it, and coffee or tea.

2 guest rooms, 1 shared bath
Moderate
No smoking. No pets.

NO. 4

*T*he Bellaire area, Houston's south-west city within a city, houses a very comfortable residential bed and break-fast. Located within five minutes from Highway 59 and ten minutes "as the crow flies" from downtown, this little jewel will put you close to the Medical Center, Rice University, and the Astrodomain. But the fact of the matter is that you may never want to leave once you stay with this gracious hostess-businesswoman, who is also a roller-coaster enthusiast. She'll entertain you with her amusement-ride stories as you sip an evening glass of wine with her by the backyard pool. An experienced traveler, she has ventured extensively through the United States in search of an ever-greater coaster thrill. Her yearning for adventure has also led her to see much of Mexico, South America, the Caribbean, and Hawaii. Wherever this charming lady has traveled, though, her home shows where her heart is.

Decorated in blues and tans, this traditional B&B has three bedrooms, one of which is a guest room decorated with Early American furniture, a rocker like Grandma used to have, and a ceiling fan. Cheery period prints add brightness to the brown-carpeted room. Guests may use the old 1950 red pay phone to make business or private calls. The hall bath is for guest use only.

The hostess is quick to note that she will accommodate larger groups by converting her sewing room and her master bedroom into guest rooms. She will even go above and beyond the call of duty by giving her spacious master bedroom to newlyweds. Called the Honeymoon Suite, the pink boudoir is equipped with a king-sized vibrating bed, soft lighting, and white eyelet ac-cessories. There's an adjoining bath and solarium that is full of live plants surrounding a hot tub. Glass patio doors here open to the patio and pool area.

Breakfast at this B&B varies from scrambled eggs to breakfast tacos and always includes croissants or sweet rolls. On occasion, a great mushroom quiche is served, depending on the schedule of both the hostess and the guests. Either coffee or tea is served, as well as juice and a variety of fresh fruit. Often, zucchini or pumpkin bread or coffee cake is provided as a special treat. If you decide to stay here, be sure to ask your hostess about all the great places to eat in Houston. She is a storehouse of information.

2 guest rooms, 2 private baths
Moderate
No smoking. No pets.

NO. 5

*I*n the west part of Houston, fifteen minutes from downtown, the weary traveler can enjoy this home away from home. Located in a quiet residential area, this Old English–style bed and breakfast houses two guest rooms upstairs (a third is being remodeled) and a bath. The downstairs, available to extended-stay guests, includes a formal living and dining room, both decorated in antique Oriental; a breakfast room that joins a traditional kitchen; and a large living area that is accessible to the shady backyard, complete with hot tub on a covered patio.

The most impressive feature of this B&B, however, is the manner in which it is furnished. One of the guest rooms is decorated with the traditional 1920s and 1930s motif in mind, with shades of Chinese influence. The ceiling fan, crocheted bed and dresser spreads, and the early century composition doll with pink chiffon and lace add a touch of the New World, while the Chinese antique bas-relief collage of satin dolls (they have human hair) adds a presence of the Old. For guests' convenience, a table and chairs are set up in each bedroom, as the hostess serves breakfast upstairs. Those staying longer come downstairs for the meal, as well as being treated to such amenities as fresh flowers and a fruit basket.

The second accommodation, furnished in a turn-of-the-century motif, would be perfect for three people, with a double wrought-iron and brass bed and a single bed. The American golden oak secretary and highboy with their

Art Nouveau influence, an antique bird cage, and nineteenth-century prints—including a 1905 Howard Christi print—provide an opportunity to step back into America's past. As an added touch, this hostess has placed a white wicker basket full of travel brochures on the desk for those wishing to learn more about Houston. Blues and greens add a coolness to this room, making it very homey and somewhat of a contrast with the earth tones of the downstairs area.

The living area is also decorated to carry through the traditional antique mood. There is an old player piano, covered with the owner's stuffed bear collection, a cozy sitting area around a large fireplace, and the television. The hostess guarantees absolute privacy if guests wish to use the romantic hot tub.

Breakfast makes staying at this B&B a true epicurean delight. There is always an egg dish (sometimes it's quiche), served with zucchini muffins, biscuits, or rolls, coffee or tea, and juice or fresh fruit. On weekends, more elaborate meals are served. You may have a chance to taste this hostess's most gourmet of breakfast foods, such as apple slices frosted with amaretto cream cheese or her wonderful pancakes with fresh blueberries. She has also been known to prepare such regional dishes as biscuits with cream gravy and breakfast tacos made with flour tortillas, eggs, Monterey Jack cheese, and spices.

2 guest rooms, 1 shared bath
Moderate
No smoking. No pets.

NO. 6
ALVIN B&B

*T*he Ewings couldn't ask for anything more than this large one-and-a-half-story contemporary B&B on a sprawling nine acres in Alvin. However, there are no oil wells here to obscure the view of the Texas countryside, which has recently been dotted with sixty young pecan trees. The owners, a mechanical engineer who specializes in real estate and a registered nurse anesthetist, obviously love their home and are happy to share their dream come true with you.

As a guest, you have free rein of the house, with its Texas-sized paneled family room, complete with big-screen television. The massive flagstone fireplace and cathedral ceiling add even more to the feeling of space. The attractive contemporary furniture contrasts well with the light carpeting and walls, adding to the warm atmosphere. In addition, the lime-green kitchen and the green and white dining area with silvery foil wallcovering open onto the den, accentuating the home's openness. After breakfast, climb the spiral staircase and enter the game room, where you can challenge the host to a game of pool. If you're saddle-sore from riding too long in Houston's rush-hour traffic, soothe your tired muscles in the hot tub in the glassed cabana. But if you choose to stay in bed until noon, your host and hostess will accommodate you. There will be no traffic noises to disturb your slumber.

You'll have two guest rooms from which to choose. The first, furnished with a king-sized bed and accessories, is decorated in shades of green with peppy striped wallpaper and has its own bath. The second, larger room has its own remote-control television and is equipped with two king-sized beds. Guests who use this room also have their own bath. For one too many people, there is a trundle bed in the game room. Three St. Bernards also live here but will be put out of sight if you don't like dogs.

**2 guest rooms, each with
private bath**

**Moderate
No restrictions**

NO. 7
BRYAN B&B

*I*f you're a Texas Aggie fan but hate the stamped-out coldness of a traditional Holiday Inn, Bryan has a guest house for you in the country. In the winter you can stand on the back patio of this ranch-style one-story and actually see the stadium over a vast expanse of Texas rural farmland. The surrounding area looks virtually untouched, much the same as when Stephen F. Austin's colonists settled here along the Brazos around 1821. You can unwind here while watching your kids fish for small fry in the private tank or study the resident oil well pump black gold in the distance.

This modern B&B, shaded by an oasis of trees, sits amid a quiet thirteen acres that can be reached only by traveling down a country graveled road. The couple who live here have five children, with a teenager and a college student residing at home. As a result, they are family oriented and welcome little ones. And rest easy if you're worried about your offspring not getting a proper breakfast. This hostess serves a full country meal of pancakes, scrambled eggs, sausage, rolls, bacon, juice, and coffee. A basket of fruit is also placed in each room.

The guest room, one of four in the home, is decorated in Early American furniture, with a double bed and matching dresser. The burgundy daybed was handmade by the hostess's grandfather fifty years ago and is still in excellent condition. Yellows and white accent the knotty pine walls, with these cheerful colors carried through to the private bath.

Guests have the run of the house, including the formal living and dining room. In fact, you are welcome to invite a small number of afternoon guests for an after-the-game conference or conversation. There is a piano in the living room that is used by the very lyrical family, whose musical background can be traced back to fathers on both sides. In fact, you can admire two ancestral fiddles that are mounted on the walls, one of which is strung with horsehair and each belonging to a father. One, however, yielded music of the Carolinas, while the other brought the Cajun two-step to Louisiana ears.

Don't leave before you have a chance to sit on the beautiful red brick patio. White wrought-iron furniture, a picnic table, park benches, a hammock, and a swing make it a perfect setting in which to have a barbecue. Oaks and elms shade the restful spot, which is dotted with flowering plants of different kinds. The kids will enjoy throwing horseshoes or playing in the grandchildren's sandbox while you turn the ribs. The only thing that could make your stay more complete is an Aggie win.

1 guest room
1 bath (in the hall but private)
Moderate
No alcohol, please

Nacogdoches

*N*acogdoches—the oldest town in Texas. That phrase just about sums up this town with the strange Indian name. According to legend, there were twin brothers, one fair, the other dark. When the old chief was dividing his domain between the brothers, one was sent east to found the town of Natchitoches, Louisiana, and the fair son founded Nacogdoches. Regardless of legend, the two towns were bound together through their colorful histories for centuries.

Natchitoches was the result of the French settling Louisiana, and they blazed a trail to Mexico to trade with Spain. The Spanish were not enthusiastic about their new neighbors and felt they should have Texas all to themselves. Consequently, in 1716 the Spanish established a mission here. It was not a success, and after Spain was ceded Louisiana in 1762, the French withdrew all efforts to settle East Texas.

The few colonists were furious at being sent to San Antonio, and finally, without permission from Spain, Gil Antonio Ibarvo and his followers resettled Nacogdoches in 1779. This historic town played a major role in Texas history. Since it was an entry post on the Camino Real, every famous and infamous person in Texas's past walked the streets of Nacogdoches. Many of

them remained here forever; the cemetery has almost as many heroes as the
State Cemetery in Austin. The Old Stone Fort that sheltered so many way-
farers and figured in many battles has been recreated on the campus of Stephen F. Austin State University from the original stones. It is well worth a
visit today, for it is a museum of early Texas. And among the museum's exhibits is an early oil rig, the first to drill in Texas soil. Across the street from
the museum is a tacky little monument to the man who brought in Texas's first
well: Lyne Taliaferro Barret. And special thanks go to Ann and Charles
Phillips, who saved another monument to Barret, his Nacogdoches home. In
this historic house is one of the best B&Bs in the Lone Star State.

BARRET HOUSE

*A*fter winding your way through the
beautiful East Texas piney woods near Nacogdoches, you come upon a Texas
pioneer cabin that rests on stone block foundations, just as it did in another
place, another time. Here lived one of the great unsung heroes of Texas,
Lyne Taliaferro Barret, or Tol, as he was affectionately called. When you see
the massive refineries of Exxon, Texaco, or Gulf, it is difficult to believe that
their predecessor lived in this humble dwelling so long ago, for Tol Barret
made the first oil strike in Texas.

You can still visit the site of the first oil well in Texas at nearly Oil Springs
if you persevere and don't let a red mud road and dense undergrowth deter
you. Pumps still chug away in the ancient field. The first steel storage tanks
are still there, and a pipe sticks out of the ground where Tol's well was completed in 1866. Tol was never able to get adequate financing for his Melrose
Petroleum Company, so Pennsylvania, rather than Texas, became the first oil-
producing state.

Tol's home was destined for destruction by its previous owner, who wanted
to use the wood for a barn. The Phillipses were appalled that such a landmark would be destroyed and tried to find a buyer. When none was forthcom-
ing, they bought it themselves, moved it to their property, and lovingly restored it. Tol would find his home much as it was before his death in 1913.

Barret House

This gem of pioneer Texas homes was originally built in the dog-run style; yet unlike the style of many cabins, its parlor was strictly a parlor, for Mrs. Tol did not allow anyone to sleep in her "settin'" room.

All of the cooking was done outside, and the Phillipses have recreated the smokehouse and even smoked their own venison as it was done on the Barret homestead. Ann also builds a fire under her big iron pot and brews and bubbles her own lye soap.

Thanks to their grandchildren, many of the Barrets's original treasures are in their home, including their marriage certificate, a portrait, and the accounts ledger. When Tol wasn't drilling for oil, he was a justice of the peace and storekeeper. His old ledger, with its neat and thorough entries, are yours for the browsing; each sale tells a story of life in Texas's oldest town.

Much could be told about the authenticity of the Barret House. A picture, "Lee and His Generals," hangs in the warming kitchen, for Tol was a captain in the Confederate Army. Tol's favorite colors were used throughout the house, and pieces were added and duplicated as closely as the grandchildren could remember their ancestors.

The B&B portion of Barret House is behind the original cabin in a replica of an addition that was no longer on the house when the Phillipses purchased it. For you, there is a parlor, a full kitchen, a bath, and a sleeping loft just as they were many years ago. A huge fireplace has an unusual brass spit that was wound up and slowly cooked the meat as it unwound. The loft has two single "eave" beds. Captain Phillips is so clever that when he found one of these rare antiques, he copied it himself to complete the decor.

Even the yard is just as the Barrets kept it, in a "swept garden." Every blade of grass was pulled out and the yard swept clean with a stick broom. Flower beds were in geometric designs, lined with ale bottles and often filled with roses. Here the Phillipses have recreated the garden, but the ale bottles have been replaced with beer bottles from the local honky-tonk. However, Ann still uses a stick broom to sweep the garden.

For the true ambience of early days in East Texas, this is the perfect B&B. It will inspire you to try that red mud road and explore the beginnings of the mighty oil industry in Texas at Oil Springs.

Captain Charles and Ann Phillips
Rt. 4, Box 9400
Nacogdoches 75961
(409) 569-1249
1 guest room, 1 bath
Moderate
No smoking. No pets.

Navasota

CASTLE BED AND
BREAKFAST

*I*n 1893 Robert Templeman, who dabbled in everything from cotton and oil to ownership of Navasota's mercantile store, gave the ultimate wedding present to his son, Ward. Robert, Ward, and Ward's bride, Annie Foster, are long gone; but the gift, an 8,000-square-foot mansion, remains, testimony to a father's love for his son.

Known today as the Castle, the newly refurbished Templeman estate has been opened by Captain Tim Urquhart and his wife Helen as Navasota's first bed and breakfast. The historic residence, once owned by Sellers Rogert and the Honorable Jimmy Grice and now sitting on only two acres of the original eleven, is virtually full of antiques. You'll take one step into the turreted mansion and know that the Urquharts and their fine furniture (it took them more thirty years to accumulate it) have finally come home.

Castle Bed and Breakfast

Tim, a retired Continental Airlines pilot, and Helen, an antiques collector, have always been in search of old buildings in need of their restoration expertise. They owned one of Navasota's old bank buildings, which they restored and sold to the Bank of Navasota. They have also added the P. A. Smith Hotel to their list of buildings that they plan to refurbish someday.

The mansion, though, is their pride and joy, as it has a history that particularly fascinated the Urquharts. Scottish-born Templeman built the home on what was once part of the Foster land grant for Ward and Annie, who lived there happily but alone after their only child died at the age of three. (There is a playroom in the attic where the little girl once played.) Local historians remember the residence as once a social center for Navasota's affluent, where garden parties frequently took place on the grounds. Today the two remaining acres are full of ageless oaks that shade the lovely mansion. Cooing mourning doves add atmosphere to this peaceful setting.

As you walk up the steps and enter the large glazed wraparound porch with 110 panes of beveled glass, you'll see amid tropical plants two antique carousel horses suspended from the ceiling. Then you enter the original parquet-floored foyer, with its fourteen-foot ceiling and an unsigned Tiffany light. The library, music room, and living room with Belgian-tiled fireplace, decorated with carved gryphon pediments, are to the right, while a truly magnificent dining room is to the left. As you have breakfast here, gaze starward to the ornate plastered ceiling that was tooled by hand before it dried. Actual paintings on canvas with Della Robbia ceiling embellishment create a true work of art. Stencils of pine cones, symbolizing wealth, decorate the tiger oak walls. Note also the original chandelier, which was later wired for electricity. After breakfast, spend some time in the music room. There's an old Edison Gem cylinder roll player and an old hand-cranked seventy-eight that still work. The radio here belonged to Tim when he was a child. In fact, on it he listened to the 1939 announcement that war had been declared.

Ask Helen to show you the "jealous husband" icebox in the "all-modern" kitchen. Ice could be loaded from the outside via a trapdoor to prevent the iceman from having to enter the house. Also see the trash disposal that enabled the trashman to empty the garbage simply by opening a little door from the outside. Then step out onto the porte cochere to see an example of opulence at its best, for even the fuse box is equipped with beveled glass.

To get to the four guest rooms, each with bath, climb the magnificent Eastlake stairway accented by a twenty-foot stained-glass window. You'll find yourself in a large upstairs parlor that opens via walk-through windows to an outdoor balcony. You'll find each guest room equally charming, decorated with light fabrics to bring out the dark richness of the Victorian furniture.

The beds in each room are the focal points. You'll have your choice of a rosewood Louisiana plantation bed, a tall four-poster, a beautifully carved half-
teaster, or a seven-and-a-half-foot carved-back bed. Helen has added family
memorabilia, from her sister's baby clothes, which are displayed on her collection of antique dolls, to a long purple petticoat that was worn by her aunt
more than seventy years ago.

Breakfast at the Castle is along continental lines, and the hosts add such
complimentaries as wine and cheese in the evening. The Urquharts will also
take you to the country club as their guests if you choose, or give you a tour
of Navasota via their 1930 Model A. I suggest that you sit in the rumble seat.
They will also pick you up at Navasota Municipal Airport if you fly in. Even
if you are just passing through, call Tim and Helen anyway. For a small fee,
they will give you a guided tour through the Castle.

1404 E. Washington
No. 1 Castle Dr.
Navasota 77868
(409) 825-8051
4 guest rooms, each with
private bath
Moderate
No children under 13. No pets.

Sam Rayburn Lake

SAM RAYBURN B&B
COLE HOUSE

*W*ithin the piney woods of the Angelina National Forest is a peaceful little getaway located on Sam Rayburn Lake. Not a traditional B&B, this is a cozy guest house large enough to accommodate several adults and a small number of well-behaved children. The 1950s furnishings are simple but comfortable, and the kitchen is equipped to prepare any dish. The setting would delight Thoreau himself, with the peaceful waters of the lake whispering promises of the really big one, and the tall shady oaks and pines promising absolute seclusion.

In fact, so private is the retreat that you won't even hear a passing train in the distance. Be sure to obtain explicit directions, because you'll find yourself traveling down country gravel roads that turn into dirt tributaries that fork and twist through the woods. Pay close attention to the number of mailboxes passed and country landmarks, for you'll pass up the "cow path" that takes you to this hidden B&B. But when you get there you will find your host and hostess well educated and accommodating. A retired owner of his own oilfield maintenance company and a registered nurse anesthetist, these two will respect your privacy, or if you choose, provide you with stimulating conversation. As for conversation pieces, you'll never have need of any, because their home, adjacent to the guest house, and their above-the-garage cache are full of family antiques and memorabilia of their twenty-two years together. Virtually every wall is full of collections, from antique spurs and horseshoes to antique cameras and straight razors to old locks and skeleton keys. If you feel like spinning a yarn, these folks will accommodate you with a nineteenth-century handmade spinning wheel, as well as an authentic flax wheel. Ask them to also show you the 1840 Golden Rod hand-maneuvered vacuum cleaner and the 1901 Edison cylinder Victrola. The collection of horse gear stems from this host's love of horses. In fact, this love led to his becoming involved with the annual San Jacinto Trail Ride of Pasadena, an event that brought him and his wife together for the first time.

As for your sleeping arrangements, the guest house has two bedrooms, each with a king-sized and a single bed, and a bathroom that is shared. The living room–kitchen combination is a good place to relax and watch the color television. The best part about the house, though, is the sunny enclosed back porch, which could be used as another sleeping area if you brought cots or sleeping bags. A couch and a single daybed are provided. This is also a perfect place to stay in the air-conditioning or central heat and read a good book if you would just as soon leave nature to the birds.

For you fishermen, the host will rent you his barge (he'll take you to all the choice fishing spots) or his fishing boat with nine-horsepower motor. If you have your own boat, you can launch it nearby. The property also has its own beach, and you can swim through deep water, though the owners will tell you to do so at your own risk.

Located in the Angelina National Forest and sandwiched between the Davy Crockett National Forest and the Sabine National Forest, this guest house will put you where Texas is its greenest. With the Big Thicket only thirty minutes south, there's no doubt that you're in Indian country. Don't miss the Alabama-Coushatta Indian Reservation between Livingston and Woodville, and catch a country music performance in George Jones's hometown of Colmesneil. The famous singer has built the Jones Country Music Park there on Route 255, where nationally known country and gospel music stars perform on the first and third Sundays from April through October. He even has RV facilities and concessions, a playground, and picnic tables. Also near here is the Ellen Trout Park, Lake, and Zoo in Lufkin, the finest small zoo of its kind in Texas, with more than three hundred birds, reptiles, and mammals.

Rt. 1, Box 258
Broaddus 75929
(409) 872-3666
Or contact Bed & Breakfast
Texas Style
4224 W. Red Bird Ln.
Dallas 75237
(214) 298-5433 or
(214) 298-8586
Guest house
Moderate
No pets

Austin, San Antonio, and the Hill Country

Austin

*F*or many years Austin was just a big country town composed mainly of government workers and college students. Everyone loved its historic buildings, funky little 1930s houses, and casual restaurants. Austin never had to worry about rush-hour traffic or smog or any of the other nasty side effects of city life. All that has changed; now, with the advent of high-tech industries in the state capital, Austin is beginning to experience the problems of rapid growth. Regardless, the Capitol building will always be beautiful, the University of Texas will continue to play football, and Austinites still love their big town.

BED & BREAKFAST OF AUSTIN

*T*he driving force behind the Texas capital's B&B society is a vivacious blonde with a lot of energy and enthusiasm for her relatively new business. This former emergency-room nurse received her B&B inspiration on a trip to Santa Fe. There her hotel room was depressing, and she accidentally discovered the numerous B&Bs in Santa Fe. She wondered why a big tourist city like Austin did not have something comparable, so she set out to remedy this situation. Kathy's spirit and determination will no doubt make Austin a major B&B town.

Kathy Smolik, director
1702 Graywood Cove
Austin 78704
(512) 441-2857

NO. 1

*I*n the Lovely West Lake Hills section of Austin is a beautiful home perched on the side of a hill with a grand view of the area. Off to one side and almost hidden from view is the fairly large guest house. Sliding glass doors open onto a flagstone patio with comfortable furniture and an enclosed swimming pool. If you hear the cooing of a turtle dove, it's because one lives in a cage next to the pool.

Inside the guest house, dark plywood paneling sets off a very large living area with wall-to-wall carpeting. The bedroom has a king-sized bed and a small bath.

Breakfast fixings are provided in the full kitchen, and you fix your own at your convenience. Also, maps and brochures about Austin are left for you to peruse.

If you are a jogger or a walker, this is a wonderful neighborhood in which to get your exercise, for the streets wind around through one of Austin's most beautiful subdivisions. West Lake Hills is close to the new shopping malls that are springing up around Austin's periphery, and the MoPac expressway is practically at your doorstep.

One of the best features of this B&B is its privacy, for you have your own little house in a lovely setting, plus a cool, breezy patio on which to enjoy balmy Austin evenings.

1 bedroom, private bath
Moderate
No pets

NO. 2

*O*ne of Kathy's most charming host homes is a lovely Victorian mansion within walking distance of UT. Built in 1907 by A. N. and Jane McCallum, this two-story Queen Anne home has been lovingly renovated and furnished with antiques. Lace curtains, etched glass (created by the owner), brass fixtures, and unique wallpapers have made this old house an Austin treasure.

Nancy and Roger Danley's B&B is an upstairs room with private bath and double bed. Tiny blue and white striped wallpaper enhances the antique armoire and dresser, and a Bentwood rocker invites you to sit a spell.

But the best part of this charming B&B is the wonderful screened porch off the bedroom. Complete with ceiling fan, comfortable lounge chairs, and potted plants, it is what Nancy calls "a read-the-Sunday-paper porch."

Breakfast is served in the big dining room, and your talented hosts will show you their Victorian dollhouse. They didn't build it for their kids, who are grown; they built it for themselves. Nancy even did a petit point rug for the tiny living room. The miniature ceiling fans stir the air, and a grandfather clock placidly ticks away. Even the attic is authentic, with teensy broken toys and Christmas decorations and a sled that was put away for the summer. It is the perfect little house in the perfect big house.

The Danleys will also accept reservations on their own if you wish to call them at (512) 451-6744.

1 bedroom, private bath
Moderate
No smoking. No children.
No pets

NO. 3

*N*ot far from the traffic of this rapidly growing major Texas city is tranquil Lake Austin. A twisting scenic drive gets you to this beautiful lake in just a few minutes, and many of Austin's retired citizens have made their homes here. Most of them have a favorite hobby, which is traveling, and your hosts in this lakeside B&B are no exception. When they are at home, this retired preacher and his wife, a former teacher, make you most welcome in their B&B.

A steep path takes you down to their house, which is practically hidden from the road. You can tell that this house is thoroughly lived in, with its numerous potted plants, projects, and comfortable furniture. Your bedroom, with its double bed and bath, are off to one side of the house, and you have lots of privacy.

Running the entire length of the rear of the house is a great porch with a magnificent view of the lake. Wind chimes tinkle gently, and tiny hummingbirds dart by in their frantic efforts to sip from the feeder.

If you want a refreshing swim in Lake Austin's cool waters, it's a mere eighty steps down to the lake (and eighty back up, of course).

1 bedroom, private bath
Moderate
No restrictions

NO. 4

*W*hen Kathy was busy getting her B&B organization set up, she found that she had more demand than she had hosts. Fortunately, her very first hostess was one of those marvelous ladies who can handle any situation. Kathy said she could call Sandra on a moment's notice, and Sandra would rearrange her schedule to accommodate anyone who wanted a B&B. Sandra is a working gal and owns a small new condo in Austin's northwest hills.

This compact dwelling has the usual living, dining, and kitchen areas, with a tiny bath downstairs and two bedrooms and a bath upstairs. Sandra's choice of decor is contemporary, with big stuffed sofas, chrome, and glass. White is Sandra's favorite color scheme, and it is carried throughout the rooms. This sparkling clean B&B has a rather spartan touch, but Sandra's guests love her warm hospitality and request her home often.

As for breakfast, it's a continental affair, and Sandra will have it set up for you whenever you wish. She's off for the office, so you'll have to get up early to visit.

One of the real pluses of B&Bs is that each one is quite individual. No matter what your accommodations are, whether elegant or basic, perched on a hill with a magnificent view or in a suburban subdivision, your B&B is very special because each host and hostess is very special. You know you'll find a warm welcome, a pleasant visit, and a sincere invitation to return again and again.

1 bedroom, shared bath
Moderate
No pets

NO. 5

*A*ustin is the "gateway to the Hill Country," and you can see why as you drive Austin's twisting and curving streets. On the edge of one of the capital's subdivisions, hidden away among many old oak trees, a lovely home hangs onto a cliff overlooking the city's rapidly growing skyline.

As you sit on the stone terrace with its spectacular view, you really feel above it all. Your private little guest house has a double bed and bath, and a fat dog named Bingo will sit up to greet your arrival. Popcorn is waiting for you on the table, and breakfast is always a gourmet treat from the Texas French Bakery or a salmon mousse and fresh fruit. Beer and soft drinks are stocked in the small refrigerator by your thoughtful hostess.

In addition to all those marvelous little amenities, you will have a hostess who is dynamite. Fran is a lobbyist and has fascinating insights into the state government. Her husband is a rock enthusiast, and all of the interesting landscaping is his handiwork. Together, they have created an ideal B&B for their lucky guests.

1 bedroom, private bath
Moderate
No pets
Contact Bed & Breakfast Texas
Style
4224 W. Red Bird Ln.
Dallas 75237
(214) 298-8586

NO. 6

*A*bout ten miles south of Austin
just off Interstate Highway 35, this B&B is away from the rush of the city
traffic yet close enough for all of the capital's wonderful attractions. There's
the Governor's Mansion, the Capitol building, the fabulous LBJ Library,
Zilker Park, and a dip in the frigid waters of Barton Springs. When the sun
goes down, 6th Street comes alive, with wall-to-wall people milling around in
the restaurants and shops. Begin with cocktails at the newly restored Driskill
Hotel and work your way down this historic area of Austin.

Situated in a fairly new subdivision, Gloria's B&B is in a contemporary
duplex with handsome modern furnishings. You will be impressed with your
hostess's choice of Hill Country art and the relaxing atmosphere of this
charming home.

This very interesting lady has traveled extensively and has lived in Washington, D.C., a city she knows intimately. Now she is the co-owner of a successful gift shop in nearby Wimberley. You'll want to take some time to make
a trip to Wimberley to visit her shop and enjoy the Hill Country ambience of
that delightful town.

The guest room has twin beds and private bath, and since Gloria works,
breakfast is continental. Gloria said she spent a miserable, lonely week in a
motel when she first moved to Austin, and after hearing about B&B, she decided to offer visitors something better. This charming hostess has certainly
fulfilled her promise.

1 bedroom, private bath
Moderate
No children. No pets.

NO. 7

*Y*ou can practically see the Capitol building from this tiny hidden subdivision, yet here is a small piece of country living just minutes from downtown. Tucked away in this hidden little suburb is a modest home with a standard facade. Inside, this charming house is spit-and-polish clean, and your bedroom with its double bed and bath is off by itself for super privacy.

Your hosts are just delightful, and this is perhaps the only B&B in Texas where you can learn to milk a goat. Yes, Nelda and Jim have a wonderful menagerie of critters. A big brown and white nanny goat named Orey (for her Oreo-cookie color) rules the animal domain. Orey is incredibly friendly and just wants her head scratched—constantly.

Following Orey around is a Barbados ram named Brother. Brother acts as if he wants affection, but he's very shy. Ducks and chickens waddle and strut around the yard, and a small spring-fed pond is filled with mammoth catfish. When the ducks are fed, the water churns as the catfish snap at the delicacies as well. Under the house, protected from the cold, is a long row of rabbit hutches filled with all varieties of bunnies. Depending on their breed, some of the fluffy little fellows have ears that flop down, and all are cuddly and adorable.

Even if you aren't wild about animals, your hosts offer a very nice B&B close to downtown Austin.

1 bedroom, private bath
Moderate
No smoking. No pets.

Bastrop

PFEIFFER HOUSE

*B*astrop, one of the oldest settlements in Texas, carries the name of Baron Felipe Enrique Neri de Bastrop, one of the best friends the Republic of Texas ever had. Though the baron's background is vague, his importance in Texas history is significant; due to his influence, Governor António María Martínez reconsidered Moses Austin's request for colonization. As a result, he made one of the most fateful decisions in Mexican history. With the arrival of the Anglos, Mexico would be only a destructible obstacle in the path of America's Manifest Destiny.

Bastrop continued to be a great friend to Stephen F. Austin and always sought legislation favorable to immigration. According to the Mexican system, Bastrop was paid by contributions from his constituents. Ironically, Texans were not as generous with their aid to their benefactor, and Bastrop died so destitute that contributions had to be solicited for his funeral. At least a city and county in the state and nation he befriended bear his name.

Bastrop is nestled among huge pine trees known as the "lost pines." These evergreens are a marooned stand of timber that was once part of the forests of East Texas. The Ice Age caused such flooding and erosion that these pines were isolated between the Gulf Coast and the Hill Country. Naturally, lumbering has been the prime industry for Bastrop.

At the turn of the century, one of the major builders in this old town was J. R. Pfeiffer. His art and handicraft can be seen in many of Bastrop's homes, but the Pfeiffer House is particularly charming, as he built it in 1901 for his bride, Freda. Known as "carpenter Gothic," the design was taken from pattern books, but Mr. Pfeiffer always added his own particular touches to his houses.

Papa and Freda would feel right at home if they came back to Pfeiffer House today. Marilyn White's touches have turned back the years. A grandfather clock marks off the passing of the years in a formal Victorian parlor. The heavy sliding doors still close off the dining room where the Pfeiffers ate herring salad at Christmastime. Delightful bric-a-brac in every nook and cranny creates a perfect Victorian decor. Marvelous old lamps with their hand-painted shades are a special delight. Not every matched pair of shades was acquired at the same place at the same time, or at the same price. Marie Renick said that the house is furnished almost exactly like Mama's. The beautiful handwork on the bullethole trim and Papa's ornate entry and dining room china cabinet are still intact and so representative of his abilities.

Marilyn offers three guest rooms, always cheerful with fresh flowers for visitors who are anxious to enjoy the ambience of the Pfeiffer House. Each room is absolutely a Victorian dream, and your room comes with a full breakfast of fresh fruit, juice, coffee, and delicious biscuits served with Eggs à la Goldenrod. (Rest easy if you're allergic to the pollen pest; only the name of the plant is borrowed!) You'll fall in love with Marilyn's egg dish, which is a delectable mixture of sausage, hard-boiled eggs, and gravy. The meal is served formally as a community affair at a prearranged time. You won't have to wait to sit down at the table, though, to have a cup of fresh coffee. The Whites serve a wake-up cup upstairs in the rooms. Afternoon homemade cookies are also provided.

1802 Main
Bastrop 78602
(512) 321-2100
3 guest rooms, 1 shared bath
Moderate
No children. No pets.
No credit cards

Fredericksburg

*T*he story of Fredericksburg is the story of German tenacity and endurance. Named for Frederick the Great of Prussia, the town was settled under the leadership of the brilliant John O. Meusebach in 1846. This former aristocrat gave up an impressive title to become the founder of the German colonies in Texas. Meusebach negotiated a treaty with the Comanches that both sides honored, and the Germans were never raided as were other settlements.

Fredericksburg has a number of special events during the year, most of which commemorate its colorful history. The Easter Fires Pageant tells the story of the Indian bonfires as Meusebach negotiated the treaty. Also fun are A Night in Old Fredericksburg and the Gillespie County Fair, and Fredericksburg is in addition the birthplace of Volkssports in America. Their Oktoberfest Walkfest is a special six-mile walking trail open to walkers of all ages at their own pace. Each year the route is changed, and people come from all over the world for this official event.

This quaint German town offers an abundance of tourist attractions and many fine restaurants. An old-time favorite for German food is the Bavarian

Inn. Fredericksburg was also the birthplace of the Texas B&B concept, and thanks to its founder, Kenn Knopp, B&Bs are rapidly expanding throughout the state.

BED AND BREAKFAST OF FREDERICKSBURG

*T*he first known B&B organization in Texas was founded in Fredericksburg by Kenn Knopp after his 1980 tour to the Passion Play at Oberammergau in Germany. Because of a hotel shortage in this ancient German town, Kenn's tour was forced to stay in private homes. What a surprise for the group! They loved their German hosts and accommodations. No one wanted a hotel room for the rest of the tour. Such enthusiasm made them agree that there was no better place to start a Texas version of B&B than Fredericksburg, the "little Europe of Texas." After a slow start, requests to become a host began to pour in. Now Kenn has to enlist the services of a computer to handle his B&B organization and has even published a monthly magazine, *Bed and Breakfast World*, with its goal of "helping to feel at home in a home away from home."

Kenn Knopp, director
307 W. Main
Fredericksburg 78624
(512) 997-4712

NO. 1

*K*enn Knopp doesn't run his own B&B, but his mother, Mina, keeps the organization in the family. Her yellow frame house was moved to this site rather recently by its previous owner, who said it was once a kindergarten. Now it is one of Fredericksburg's most delightful host homes.

Mina's choice of decor is charming. Old fainting couches, lovely figurines, and other wonderful antiques reflect her good taste. Many of her treasures, such as an old violin, are framed creatively, as are a number of detailed trapunto pieces (tapestry quilting) that Mina has worked herself. Many collectibles fill the den, and canaries trill sweetly in their cages among the African violets.

Two guest rooms are also beautifully decorated in antiques, old-fashioned wallpaper, elaborate silk draperies, and interesting bric-a-brac. The two bedrooms share a bath, and you cannot help but realize that Mina has put a great deal of thought into her guests' comfort.

The breakfast part of Mina's B&B is served on the covered portion of the delightful patio. A ceiling fan stirs the Hill Country breeze as you partake of Fredericksburg pastries. A picket fence, numerous potted plants, St. Francis of Assisi, and even merry little gnomes add to the warmth of your welcome in this special garden.

2 bedrooms, 1 bath
Moderate
No smoking. No pets.

NO. 2

*I*f you like to square dance, you'll love this B&B host and hostess. Edna and Henry have a closet full of their elegant and elaborate dance costumes and will entertain you with amusing anecdotes about their favorite hobby. Also, Edna's and Henry's ancestors were early Fredericksburg settlers, and this delightful couple can tell fascinating stories of these indomitable German immigrants. As do many of Fredericksburg's citizens, Edna and Henry speak German, so their home is popular with foreign guests.

This B&B is not one of the historic structures of the town; in fact, the single-story stucco house was built in 1949. But a historic building is not a prerequisite for a successful B&B. Edna's home shows much love and attention, with lots of handsome porcelains and other bibelots among comfortable overstuffed furniture.

You can have your choice of two handsome rooms, one with a double bed or one with two twin beds, and the bath is between the bedrooms. The guest rooms are furnished in a continuation of Edna's bric-a-brac, which gives the rooms a very personal touch.

Breakfast is a production, and you are lavished with German sausage rolls, poached eggs, steaming oatmeal, or anything you wish at any time you wish. Edna serves her savory repast in her small formal dining area, and you will be well fortified to visit the many Fredericksburg tourist attractions.

2 bedrooms, 1 bath
Moderate
No smoking. No pets.

NO. 3

*M*ost of the stone farmhouses around Fredericksburg date back to pioneer days when settlers were given

ten acres outside of town and a town lot. However, people are beginning to
construct new houses in the same style as the originals, for so many are finding this quaint German town so relaxing that they want to live here, too.

Jenny and Werner's farm is about ten miles outside of Fredericksburg, and
they are still working on their large two-story home. This friendly young
couple have turned their charming guest cottage into a very private B&B.

The one large room has a fireplace with a wood-burning stove to keep out
the chill on winter days, and a paddle fan adds atmosphere in the summer.
Cathedral ceilings, a queen-sized bed, a kitchenette, and a large bath are all
part of this out-of-the-way B&B.

If you want the total bucolic scene, swing contentedly on the porch as fat
cows and Barbados sheep graze contentedly on the lawn.

1 bedroom, private bath
Moderate
No smoking. No pets.

NO. 4

*I*f you have ever wondered what
schoolteachers do when they aren't grading papers, just request this B&B.
Carol and Joe are not only remodeling their garage into guest quarters, but
they are also avid summer travelers. Ask to share their videotape of a recent
European jaunt—staying in B&Bs, of course.

This home is still on the fringe of civilization, so you can sit in the huge
backyard and enjoy a Hill Country view. Quails nest under the shady trees,
armadillos stroll casually across the yard, and deer stop to nibble a hedge
or two.

Inside the house is a room with a private entrance as well as a private
bath. Joe and Carol do not care for air-conditioning. They realize that most
people are totally addicted to frigid air, though, so you have your own unit.

In the rear of the house, the two-story garage has become another little
world of B&B. Upstairs, ceiling fans whir over a double and two twin beds,

and there is a window air-conditioning unit. A claw-foot tub dominates the bath, and breakfast is placed in your own ice chest. If you like the laziness of a porch swing, you'll love this two-seater with its view.

Even though a stairway connects the upstairs and downstairs units, each floor can be shut off for total privacy. For two groups traveling together, the stairway is a real convenience. The downstairs unit has a full kitchen plus and washer and dryer.

Carol and Joe have no objections to children, and there is even a giant swing set in the shady backyard for active little bodies. Also in the yard is a majestic 1950 Dodge that these educators still love and drive. They also love old wood, and the yard has stacks of interesting salvaged pieces to use in their remodeling projects. Get Joe to spend a few minutes telling about his acquisitions. You may think of it as junk lumber, but those old boards are actually history lessons.

3 bedrooms, 2 baths
Moderate
No smoking. No pets.

NO. 5

*O*ne of Fredericksburg's favorite signs is Willkommen, and it doesn't take a linguist to figure out that this is German for "welcome." When you drive out to Bob and Nan's farm, this familiar greeting stands by the driveway. Not only are B&B guests welcome at this lovely farm, but so are a flock of geese, domestic rabbits, two South American llamas, Nubian goats, a mutt, and numerous cats. Also racing out to greet you will be Willie and Hilary, two gorgeous English sheepdogs. Hilary is so beautiful that she goes to dog shows, but she'd much rather wallow in the mud.

Your hosts are truly fascinating people. Nan teaches weaving, quilting, and cooking. An antique spinning wheel in her workshop is still used to spin her own yarn. Nan's workshop has myriads of projects awaiting time for this busy lady to complete them—after she tends the rabbits and milks the goats.

Have you ever seen eight thousand tomato plants? For years Bob grew exotic orchids in British Columbia, but now he's offering his homegrown big delicious tomatoes for sale. All you have to do is come out and pick 'em yourself. This interesting man is an avid and experienced horticulturist, and his greenhouse is now being used for his latest project, macrobiotic vegetables. A true gentleman and a scholar, Bob lives by these words: "Every day that I am allowed to live, I have resolved to provide some enjoyment for someone that they could not otherwise have afforded."

One of the guest rooms in this wonderful household looks out on the rock terrace with its lovely swimming pool. (Watch out for Hilary; she's a fiend for water.) Bob also added another special touch with a shower for two in the bath. With its twin beds, this guest room is in a wing off the main house. You can also take your choice of rooms with double or king-sized beds.

After a morning dip, when you hear the clang of the iron triangle, it's time for a full breakfast. Even if you can afford a hundred such retreats, Bob has kept his resolve to provide enjoyment. We would all do well to live by his words.

3 bedrooms, 3 baths
Moderate
No pets

NO. 6

A long, long time ago, Fredericksburg was a tiny farming community of frugal Germans striving to prosper on crops grown on the rocky Hill Country soil. Every Saturday they arrived in town with their goods and produce for market day. Rather than make the tedious journey back to the farm and another trek into town for Sunday church, many of the pioneer families built their primitive version of a townhouse. A one- or two-room basic cottage with a sleeping loft became the farmers' "Sunday house." Fortunately, a great many of these charming little Sunday houses are still in use on the sides of Fredericksburg's busy wide streets. They give the town the atmosphere of a dollhouse village.

During the 1880s, Christian and Magdalena Vogel bought a town lot valued at $200 and began their one-room board and batten Sunday house. At completion, the compact house was given a coat of pale green paint. Mama and Papa Vogel slept downstairs, and the six little Vogels shared the sleeping loft. Succeeding tenants painted the house every color from canary yellow and fire-engine red to purple. At some date (perhaps 1907), embossed metal siding was added and is still there.

Marilynne and her late husband, Randolph, purchased the Vogel house in 1976, and Randolph poured his time and love into the historic little home. They found old wooden windows with imperfect glass, wooden doors of the period, and even handmade bricks to make their addition in the rear compatible with the original building.

The addition with its private entrance is now one of Fredericksburg's most charming B&Bs, and its hostess is one of Fredericksburg's most charming ladies. Your bedroom and bath are delightful, with pineapple wallpaper, a claw-foot tub, and a comfortable king-sized bed. A sunny enclosed porch with rocking chairs looks out onto fruit trees in the backyard, and you even have the use of a deck and hot tub!

The rest of Marilynne's home is a treasure as well. She now uses the loft where the little Vogels slept as her bedroom, and Papa and Mama Vogel's room is a kitchen and dining room. Jars of canned peaches on the shelves and baskets everywhere complete the country decor. Randolph made the door to the bath a collage of wooden spools, blocks, drapery rings, and other odd items, even acorns. Breakfast is always in the small dining room with Marilynne's collection of tealeaf ironstone.

Visitors to the Vogel house must really enjoy their stay, for Marilynne says of her guests, "Beautiful people are so hard to forget."

1 bedroom, private bath
Moderate
No smoking. No children
under 7.

NO. 7

*O*n the outskirts of this all-time favorite Texas tourist town is one of the most beautiful homes in the Hill Country. It was built about 1860 but enlarged and modernized to become featured in many magazines. On the spacious grounds not far from the main house is an old stone barn more than a hundred years old. From the exterior, the barn remains totally unchanged; but inside is a charming guest house with a distinctive pioneer ambience.

Rough wood walls and a brick floor polished to perfection add to the downstairs decor. Even the sunken tub in the tiny bath is brick. Rafters cross the high ceiling, and a steep narrow staircase takes you to a cozy sleeping loft with twin beds.

In the kitchen-bath (you have to see it to understand this quaint arrangement) a small wood-burning iron stove squats solidly in a corner. It actually works, but don't worry—the only wood you'll have to haul is what you burn in the fireplace. Your hostess brings in your breakfast. This ancient appliance was a gift from Grandfather, who made his living as an early-days stove salesman.

Other little personal touches add to the warmth of this antique B&B. A childish sampler on the wall of the parlor admonishes, "Do you love life? Then do not waste time for that is what life is made of." It is no wonder that this little getaway is one of the most popular B&Bs in Fredericksburg.

1 bedroom, 1 bath
Moderate
No smoking. No small children.
No pets

Fredericksburg Number 7

NO. 8

*S*itting handsomely on top of a scrub-oak knoll, framed and enhanced by the native limestone fence and walk, this turn-of-the-century home is a B&B favorite. Your hostess did not restore this 1898 Victorian cottage, but Isabel has certainly added her charming personal touches.

The large bedroom with its beadboard walls and ceilings is the favorite of the two guest rooms, probably because it has a double bed. Polished bare floors are covered with scatter rugs, and antique furniture goes with the age of the house. This guest room shares the bath across the hall with a smaller guest room that has twin spool beds with funky calico sheets. A marble washstand, brass lamps, and tiny floral wallpaper give the bath a Victorian touch.

Isabel's sitting room, with its adjoining yellow and white kitchen, is contemporary and comfortable. Breakfast is served at a big round lazy-susan table or on a sunny brick patio.

When you enter the beautiful leaded-glass front door of Isabel's B&B, you will find Fredericksburg's famous hospitality at its best.

2 bedrooms, 1 bath
Moderate
No smoking. No small children.
No pets

NO. 9

*T*his darling little one-room B&B guest house is brand-spanking new, but it has all the charm and ambience of the old Sunday houses, for the style is identical. A small painted heart on the rusty-red door gives the traditional Fredericksburg welcome, and as you enter this dollhouse, you know that your hostess richly deserves accolades for her career as an interior designer.

Cottage curtains, a plaid sleeper sofa, and handsome bedspreads for twin beds are predominantly a rich dark blue. An antique blue and white quilt on the wall has been hung with a distinctive flair, and a mirrored country primitive wardrobe adds an impressive touch. Even though it would be a bit snug, this decorative B&B will accommodate four, and it is within easy walking distance of downtown.

1 bedroom, 1 bath
Exclusive
No smoking. No children.
No pets

NO. 10

*O*n a secluded back street on an even more secluded lot is a sturdy 1871 rock house built in the design of the early "dog-run" homes. In those cabins, rooms opened from each side of the house onto a wide hall that was roofed but had no rear or front walls. The effect was wonderful in summer for cross-ventilation, but it must have been extremely nippy on frosty days. Dog-run houses were suitable only for areas with relatively mild winters. Families cooked and dined and visited in the dog-run. They may have had a formal parlor in one of the rooms, but the everyday business of living was in the open area between the rooms. And yes, dogs (and every other farm animal) ran through this early version of a family room.

At this dog-run B&B house, progress has arrived and closed in the dog-run to make a lovely entry and dining area. If you come in by the front door, a stuffed duck, mounted in flight, seems ready to honk a friendly greeting. On the back, a wreath of grapevines nests a few guinea hens.

The furnishings of this great little B&B are almost authentic to the original decor. A fireplace, bare floors, stone walls, and beamed ceilings are authentic. The early homes probably even had the Victorian chairs and a big bearskin rug stretched out in front of the fireplace. Early settlers might have cooked over the kitchen fireplace, and the one in this B&B is still workable. Every modern kitchen convenience, though, is at your disposal.

The one bedroom has two antique double beds, but furnishings are sparse and rather austere. Frugal pioneers did not waste money on frivolities. Bathrooms were certainly not built in, either, but here one entire room was turned into a bath so large that a massive pine armoire seems right in place. The clawfoot tub is painted blue, and there is even a shower.

For a blend of the old and the new, this wonderful B&B is difficult to beat. For privacy, you have a world all to yourselves. This is definitely one of Fredericksburg's finest B&B accommodations.

1 bedroom, private bath
Exclusive
No pets

NO. 11

*N*ot all of the guest houses on the Fredericksburg B&B circuit are Sunday houses or German-style architecture. Not far from downtown, with its gingerbread trim, tin roof, and bay window, a small red cottage definitely has a Victorian flair.

The interior consists of three spacious rooms plus a bath, and all are decorated in "country" decor. In fact, this ideal B&B is affectionately referred to as the "calico house." Lacy cottage curtains, gaily patterned wallpaper, and a lovely old quilt make the bedroom with its double bed delightful. In the sitting room, a stuffed sofa unfolds to make a queen-sized bed, making this guest cottage perfect for four.

A full kitchen with a dinette is supplied with breakfast fixings, so you are on your own to eat when you please. Holding the door open into the small entry hall is an irate black cat with emerald-green eyes, just another touch that gives this B&B a calico touch.

There are no phones or television, but who cares? You came to experience the charm of Fredericksburg, and this Victorian dollhouse is the perfect headquarters.

1 bedroom, private bath
Exclusive
No children. No pets.

NO. 12

*J*ust twenty-two miles from Fredericksburg is Kerrville, home of the fabulous Cowboy Artists Museum, and off this highway is one of the town's outstanding B&Bs. It's in a traditional rock farmhouse, but Helen's home is brand-new. It just blends into the scenery so perfectly that it seems that it has been there forever.

Helen has put a lot of thought into her home to maintain the ambience of a German pioneer-style house. Natural woodwork, etched-glass doors, lace curtains, and a big stone fireplace create a warm, homey atmosphere. Guests immediately feel welcome. Just off the main room is a delightful dining area with the Hill Country spread out before you.

The upstairs guest room is probably the largest of all the B&Bs. At first it seems that Helen has made the entire area into just one huge room, but behind this room is a "dormitory" filled with beds that make it ideal for a large group. The whole upstairs is carpeted wall to wall, with a Fredericksburg double bed and dresser. An antique trunk serves as a table, and you can watch television as you relax in a Bentwood rocker.

Helen's rancher neighbor goes in for exotic game, so you just might see a longhorn steer, a buffalo, or even an antelope grazing in the nearby pasture.

**1 bedroom, 1 bath,
plus "dormitory"
Moderate
No smoking**

NO. 13
RIVERBEND FARMS

"*P*arsley, sage, rosemary, and thyme." No, it's not Scarborough Fair, just a marvelous Hill Country B&B. Off the Kerrville highway you'll see a modest sign pointing to Riverbend Farms, and a mile or two down the road you go off the beaten path to Lynn and Don's restored German farmhouse and all of its charming outbuildings.

From afar, the backyard appears to be a manicured formal garden. But instead of a profusion of old-fashioned flowers, beds are bordered in parsley, and every variety of seasoning dear to a chef's heart grows here. Open the door of the tiny rock barn, and hanging from its high rafters you will see all sorts of flowers, peppers, and herbs hanging up to dry. Some of these aromatic sprigs will be turned into Lynn's lovely dried flower arrangements and others gathered into fragrant sachets. Be sure to visit her workshop adjacent to the barn and see samples of her talent.

After a stroll through the carefully nurtured herb garden, rest a spell on the patio and savor the delicate aroma of mint, chives, and other delicious flavors growing so close by.

Lynn and Don have moved in the guest quarters in the form of another old German farmhouse. This is one of the "dog-run" homes, and it is charmingly furnished in iron beds, antique quilts, and primitive chests and chairs. Not only are the house and garden wonderful, but Lynn and Don are very interesting people, and your visit with them will be unforgettable.

Lynn Watt, innkeeper
Kerr Rt., Box 53
Fredericksburg 78624
(512) 997-9031
4 bedrooms, 1 shared bath
Moderate
No children. No pets.

NO. 14

*E*lvis, pony tails, and tons of petticoats may have been the signs of the times during the 1950s, but a real fashion status symbol for ladies of any age was a purse signed "E.C." This was the famous Collins bag, designed and produced by Enid Collins. These box purses were painted, sequined, and jeweled in every possible combination. Some were owls, some were doves, and others sported all manner of beasties. The fad ran its course, but you can still buy a Collins bag. It won't be signed "E.C.," for Enid sold the company. Now this incredibly talented lady runs a B&B in an 1892 Fredericksburg rock house.

The old loft sleeping rooms are now two charming guest rooms, one with twin beds and the other with a double bed. Quilts, braided rugs, antique furnishings, and even bright *molas* (Panama Indian needle art) make the rooms warm and inviting.

Downstairs is a collector's delight: Enid's creations in fabric, her various renditions of St. Francis of Assisi, and a collection of pewter plates that she designed for Fredericksburg. A hand-carved Noah's Ark, complete with pairs of God's creatures, is the work of one of Enid's friends, as are several other bibelots in this marvelous living room.

Enid's own bedroom is also her workshop, with many of her projects under way. She still has a few of her Collins purses, in case you are too young to have owned one. They aren't for sale, but Enid will be glad to show them to you. The designer said that occasionally she finds a signed bag at garage sales. Who knows? Perhaps Enid's purses will be true collectors' items; if you own one, best you save it!

Near the big house is an old log cabin being used by Enid's son—a jewelry designer—as an office. Another stone building is his workshop. The entire family is very talented, and they also run a gift shop in Fredericksburg.

A small garden and your own private tennis court complete this marvelous B&B and make you really glad that Enid shares her home and her talents with her lucky guests.

2 bedrooms, 1 bath
Moderate
No smoking. No pets.

NO. 15

*T*exas is indeed fortunate that most of the old pioneer rock homes in Fredericksburg are still in use. Seeing their tin roofs and sleeping lofts, you cannot help but absorb the flavor of early Texas-German life when you are a guest in one of these marvelous little houses. The simplicity and sturdiness of their construction and furnishings provide an obvious clue to the no-nonsense nature of their original owners. It is like a living history lesson, and we are indebted to Fredericksburg's hosts for opening these homes as B&Bs.

A Houston physician and his wife have restored a Sunday house and turned it into a perfect B&B only a block off Main Street. Bare floors with scatter rugs, open beamed ceilings, and a large fireplace are typical of these early homes, and even electricity and indoor plumbing do not detract from their pioneer flavor.

In this Sunday house, rocking chairs gather around the stone fireplace in the parlor, and a ferocious bearskin rug sprawls on the floor. Modern appliances in the full kitchen blend in with its rough-cut cabinets and smooth rock floors. A lovely stained-glass door panel in a grape design softens the stark simplicity of the cottage.

The bedroom upstairs has two three-quarter beds covered with blue and white quilts of some bygone era. One of the primitive antique beds is authentic, and the other is a copy. Only a trained and experienced eye can tell which is the real thing. A German country-style armoire is the closet, and the only Victorian touch is a dear little brass baby bed.

A narrow front porch behind the white picket fence is a pleasant place from which to watch Fredericksburg's busy citizens pass in review.

1 bedroom, 1 bath
Exclusive
No smoking. No small children.
No pets

NO. 16
GASTHAUS ON DER
HAUPTSTRASSE

*O*ne of the best Main Streets in Texas is in Fredericksburg. Each side of this wide, busy section of U.S. Highway 290 is lined with historic buildings that have been carefully and beautifully restored. Gift and antique shops, restaurants, and stores do a fantastic business catering to the numerous tourists the town attracts. Also on the list of major attractions is the fantastic Nimitz Museum, now a part of the state's Parks and Wildlife Department.

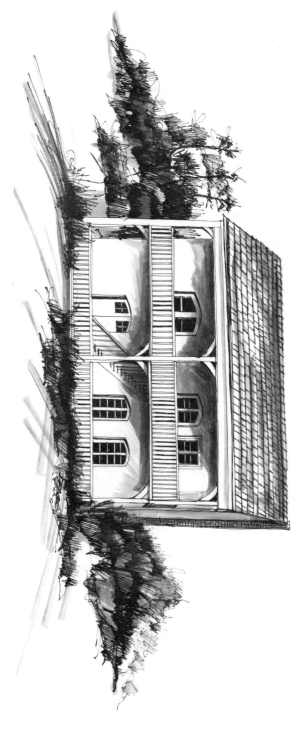

Gasthaus on der Hauptstrasse

Just across from the Nimitz Museum is the first two-story solid stone residence built in Fredericksburg. Friedrich Kiehne and his wife, Maria, began their home in 1805 and added four more rooms in 1860. Now a second Maria owns the Kiehne home. Even though it is still furnished in wonderful Texas primitives or German country-style antiques, the first Maria would be green with envy over the modern kitchen, inside plumbing, and air-conditioning.

Much has been written about this pioneer home and its marvelous restoration by the second Maria, and every word is glowing praise for her notable accomplishment. This talented B&B hostess is also the owner of a successful sportswear shop and speaks six languages.

From Main Street the Gasthaus looks small and compact. However, it is a ten-room house with a beautiful backyard and parking in the rear. When you enter, your first reaction is to gasp, "How absolutely wonderful!" The front bedroom has a magnificent brass and porcelain double bed and a brass stove. The other furnishings are lovely but are overwhelmed by the bed and stove. Cupids fly over the hearth in the parlor, and an unusual fire screen was designed especially for this room. Maria has placed many fine antiques in this grand little parlor, and you will appreciate them all.

The dining area has a long German country-style table that came from nearby Comfort, another Texas German settlement. Maria said the table was even older than this house.

A smaller back bedroom is warm and homey with its spool bed. This very handsome double bed is one of the favorite antiques in the Gasthaus. With its thick white walls and pine beamed ceilings, antique colorful quilts, and precious antiques, you could not ask for a better B&B anywhere.

An outside stairway leads to another wonderful little suite upstairs. Here are two bedrooms, a bath, and a kitchenette. With the very personal touches by Maria, it is as charming as the downstairs suite. This gem of B&Bs is perfect for two couples or four couples, as the upper and lower suites are connected by an inside stairway as well. Breakfast is left in the refrigerator, and you can fix your own whenever you wish.

Life may have been hard for those early German pioneers, but Texas is grateful for the rich heritage they left behind and to women like Maria McDonald who share it with us.

Maria McDonald, innkeeper
(512) 997-4916 or 997-9624
4 bedrooms, 2 baths
Exclusive
No smoking. No pets.

BARON'S CREEK INN

*I*t has to be a special building for famous Hill Country artist Charles Beckendorf to sketch it, and Baron's Creek Inn is special indeed. So, as a gift to the Switzers, Beckendorf gave them a wonderful line drawing of their inn. Naturally it has a place of honor in the entry hall.

This 1911 German house was built by Max Eckert, and Max was so proud of his accomplishment that he had his name stamped in the concrete step. Behind the big house is a small Sunday house where the Eckerts lived until they were affluent enough to build a "proper" home. The Switzers have turned this little Sunday house into a spacious suite, tastefully furnished to accommodate four. Children are welcome, too.

Also on the grounds is the old circular water tank with its windmill that still pumps water to water the lawn. Max hung cured meat in the bottom of the tank and also practiced enology (winemaking). The shady grape arbor that the German settler planted is still a welcome retreat during hot Hill Country afternoons. The Switzers are emulating Max and planting grapes as well. However, the Switzers' vineyards are out of town on their farm. In a few years Sandy and Spencer hope to be selling grapes to the booming Texas wineries.

When you turn the doorbell on the inn's etched-glass door, you are welcomed into a wide hall with steep narrow stairs leading to the inn's two suites. The Sunrise and Sunset Suites are appropriately on the east and west side of the house. Each has a large parlor with a sofa that makes into a queen-sized bed, a separate bedroom, a big kitchen, and a bath.

The inn may be 1911 vintage, but air-conditioning, ceiling fans, television, and microwave ovens are now standard in the suites and the Sunday house. Yet, beadboard ceilings, natural wood trim, antique furnishings, and Victorian light fixtures give the inn its proper ambience. Walls are painted in soft colors rather than wallpapered, and the usual tons of Victorian bric-a-brac have yet to be added.

If you have one of the upstairs suites, you can not only relax in the restful grape arbor but also sit on the wide verandas on both floors. You won't see the busy world of Main Street, but you didn't come to Baron's Creek Inn for a tourist crush. You came for a hideaway, yet all of this peace and tranquility is only a few blocks from the shops, restaurants, and bakeries. A perfect combination of both worlds is here at the lovely Baron's Creek Inn.

**Sandy and Spencer Switzer,
innkeepers
110 E. Creek
Fredericksburg 78624
(512) 997-9398
3 suites, 3 baths
Exclusive
No smoking. No guests
under 14 upstairs. No pets.
Two nights required
during special events**

BE MY GUEST

*R*eservations for the B&Bs in Fredericksburg may also be made through this organization.

**Helen Taylor
330 W. Main
Fredericksburg 78624
(512) 997-7227**

Llano

BADU HOUSE

*W*hen you first see the Badu House, this stern, imposing brick and granite building may not be how you imagined a country inn to look. That is because it was originally built in 1891 as the First National Bank of Llano. The builders probably hoped that its stern facade would inspire trust and confidence in Llano's citizens. The trust and confidence only lasted until 1898, when the bank failed and the building was sold at auction to N. J. Badu. Always known as "Prof," this French entrepreneur made the building a home for his wife and two girls.

Badu and his descendants lived in the house for more than eighty years. Already placed on the National Register of Historic Places and a Texas historical landmark when Ann and the late Earl Ruff purchased it in 1980, the Badu House began another era as a country inn.

The exterior of the Badu House is unchanged and still a solid block of brick with its unique granite checkerboard trim, but when you open the heavy doors with their beautiful stained-glass panels, you are transported back to great-grandmother's life and times. Victorian wallpaper in shades of blue and pink takes your breath away with its striking patterns, and bric-a-brac and old photographs add numerous touches of charm. "Prof" himself beams down from a portait over the fireplace, no doubt quite pleased with his home's elegant transformation.

Upstairs, oak panels that separated lawyers' offices in 1891 now line the hallway for eight charming guest rooms and seven baths for overnight guests. Furnished in antiques, collectibles, and funky wallpaper, the rooms offer a delightful return to the past.

One of the most beautiful features of the Badu House is the bar in the Llanite Club. Hearty drinks are served on slabs of polished llanite, a rare opaline mineral with large blue quartz crystals that sparkle in the sunlight. Llanite is found only in Llano County, and this may be the largest display of this unusual stone in the world.

Ann Ruff, innkeeper
601 Bessemer
Llano 78643
(915) 247-4304
Moderate
8 bedrooms, 7 baths
No children under 14
No pets

New Braunfels

*T*his quaint German community had its beginning a long time ago, in 1845, when the aristocratic Prince Carl of Solms-Braunfels arrived with the first contingent of German pioneers. The prince did not remain in Texas very long; he returned to Braunfels on the Lahn River in Germany to his fiancée, Sophia. But it was here in New Braunfels that the German heritage in Texas had its start, and it has since become a proud part of Texas history.

With its colorful past, its beautiful clear Comal and Guadalupe Rivers, its good food, and many celebrations, this old German town is now one of the state's best tourist attractions. Numerous motels and two historic hotels, the Faust and the Prince Solms, are often filled for special events weekends. The granddaddy of all Texas celebrations, Wurstfest, draws thousands of visitors during the first two weeks of November.

Of course, tubing and canoeing on the Comal and Guadalupe Rivers are a Central Texas tradition, but New Braunfels has also preserved its rich history in the very fine Sophienburg Museum, named for Prince Carl's fiancée. Be sure to take the walking tour of the many historic pioneer homes and buildings that endure.

Good restaurants are a major part of New Braunfels. Krause's is another Texas tradition, and Wolfgang's Keller cannot be equalled for continental cuisine. For shoppers, the town is a veritable storehouse of antiques. So no matter what your interest, New Braunfels has it all. And what better way to enjoy your visit than to stay in a friendly B&B?

NO. 1

*I*f you are an antiques buff, you'll love this B&B. Esther, your hostess, owns a delightful antique shop in New Braunfels, and all of her guests receive a 10 percent discount on anything in her store, no matter the size or price. Primitive handmade furniture, collectibles, vintage clothes, and old hats are just a few of the shop's numerous wares.

Esther and Wendall own a subdivision all their own, and one of the fairly recent houses in it is their home. It's an easy three miles on the outskirts of town. Comfortable modern furniture blends nicely with early Texas pieces in the large living room. A pine wardrobe is filled with more of Esther's fragile antique lingerie and funky hats from bygone days.

The guest room with private bath is charming. Tiny floral moiré taffeta wallpaper is complemented by a pom-pom spread on the brass double bed. You can make your own pom-pom spread by cutting circles of fabric, gathering the edges into a small bag, pressing them flat, and then sewing hundreds of them together in the color pattern of your choice. Esther didn't create this particular pom-pom spread, but she did cane the room's antique rocker. Lace curtains and a ceiling fan add to the decor of this lovely room.

Breakfast is a feast of German wurst, or perhaps breakfast tacos served with jelly made from the grapes in Esther's yard and honey from her Kansas farm. So even if you aren't interested in antiques, you will still find this B&B a very special treat.

1 bedroom, 1 bath
Moderate
Smoking on porch only. No small
children. No pets.
Contact Bed & Breakfast Texas
Style
4224 W. Red Bird Ln.
Dallas 75237
(214) 298-8586

NO. 2

*T*he shortest river in Texas doesn't flow into another larger river; it goes nowhere. The spring-fed Comal River just makes a complete circle through New Braunfels, and its "chutes" provide great entertainment for those who go tubing pell-mell with the crystal clear water that races over rocks and boulders. Shrieks of excitement and fun echo along this river's banks as kids from five to sixty-five "shoot the chutes." Jillions of tubes carry bodies in every size and shape on the Comal's circuit.

Rustic old Camp Warneke has been a tourist haven forever, and its basic accommodations are very popular. Directly across from this New Braunfels landmark is a real B&B treat and a hideaway well worth discovering. This small river cottage has two bedrooms and one bath, but with the sofa bed, six guests can be made comfortable. Rattan furniture in the living room adds to the vacation atmosphere, and your hostess stocks the refrigerator in the small kitchen with your heart's desire for breakfast.

The main charm of this idyllic cottage is its wonderful deck, which runs the entire length of the back of the house. A wind chime tinkles lightly with a

Hill Country breeze, carefree laughter and splashing sounds resound off the Comal, and shady trees, ferns, and big pots of glorious geraniums hide this perfect retreat from the hot Texas sun.

If you must have some sort of exercise, try the dartboard. Downtown New Braunfels is also within easy walking distance. Here you have the best of both worlds of New Braunfels—the river and the town—and you don't have to work at either of them.

2 bedrooms, 1 bath
Moderate
No smoking. No pets.
Contact Bed & Breakfast Hosts
of San Antonio
Laverne Campbell, director
166 Rockhill
San Antonio 78209
(512) 824-8036

Salado

*J*ust off the rushing world of Interstate Highway 35 is the tiny peaceful hamlet of Salado. If you knew nothing of Texas history and were just looking at a highway map, you would think there was absolutely no reason to detour here. But Salado has been hosting famous guests for more than 150 years. Before the Spanish arrived in Texas, Indians camped by the creek that gave Salado its name. Spanish explorers found the water of the small stream salty and named the pleasant campground Salado, the Spanish word for "salty." The legend of buried Spanish gold persists till this day.

When the Anglos settled on the banks of Salado Creek, it became an important stagecoach stop, and the town even received several votes as the site of the University of Texas. The inn once resounded with the voices of Sam Houston, Robert E. Lee, Ulysses S. Grant, and many other great names in history. Homes and stores grew up around the coach stop, and Salado became a prosperous community. The era of railroads bypassed Salado, however, and for a long time all that remained were remnants of the historic inn and a few early homes.

Salado was caught in time, and even the interstate did not disturb its serenity. The old inn became a modern motel, a famous dress shop opened, along with several antique shops, but the town has remained a restful haven from hectic city life. You can return to the days of long ago with a visit to the B&B homes, all of which have been a part of Salado since its beginnings.

INN AT SALADO

*T*he Orgain House, built in 1873, is now a wonderful little country inn. This historic old home was modernized and covered with asbestos siding, and to qualify for its Texas historical medallion, all the siding will have to be removed and rotten timbers replaced. At today's horrendous cost of restoration, this monumental undertaking may be in the distant future.

Meanwhile, Larry and Cathy Sands have done wonders. The siding is a soft light blue, and the rooms are all furnished in beautiful antiques. Oriental rugs cover the polished floors, and there is an old piano in the parlor just waiting for you to play a tune.

Rooms in this old home are large and airy and named for early Salado settlers. Downstairs, the handsome Levi Tenney and G. Washington Bains rooms both have double beds and share a bath. General G. Armstrong Custer wasn't in Salado long enough to settle down, but he was a guest at the old stage stop, so he rightfully deserves this room with private bath, queen-sized bed, and queen-sized hide-a-bed named for him.

The upstairs of the Inn at Salado has been remodeled into two lovely suites. The Welborn Barton Suite can accommodate six guests with its king-sized bed and two queen hide-a-beds. The A. J. Rose Suite has a queen-sized bed, as well as one queen-sized hide-a-bed. So if you have a party of eighteen people who want to enjoy the idyllic atmosphere of one of Texas's most famous stage stops, you can rent the entire Inn at Salado.

You will love the antique furnishings of the Inn at Salado. Quilts hang from the walls and cover the beds. Lace curtains adorn the windows. Games are on the tables of the parlors in the upstairs suites, and interesting and unusual bric-a-brac decorates the rooms. Perhaps the best feature of the Inn at Salado is that each of the antiques is for sale. If you fall in love with your room, you can just take it home with you!

A continental breakfast is served in the informal dining room, or you can take your coffee out on the porch and watch visitors stroll to the antique shops or the historic homes in this little town that time forgot.

**Larry and Cathy Sands,
innkeepers
N. Main at Pace Park
Salado 76571
(817) 947-8200
3 bedrooms, 2 suites, 4 baths
Exclusive
No smoking. No children under
10. No pets.**

GUEST QUARTERS OF BARTON HOUSE

*O*nce upon a time Salado was the seat of learning in Texas, and Salado College was the reason why many families settled here. It was known for its outstanding educational facilities from the time of its founding in 1859, and average enrollment reached 250 students. In 1885 the college property was turned over to the officials of the Salado public schools, but Salado College was unique in that it operated for twenty-four years with tuition as its sole source of income.

The Bartons originally came from South Carolina via Burnet County to Salado with the purpose of enrolling their children in the famous college. They built a stone six-room home in 1866 and added more rooms and porches in the 1870s. On the ground level, the addition served as a root cellar and a summer kitchen, and legend has it that both Sam Houston and George Armstrong Custer were entertained in this room.

Unusual features of the house were the solid rock staircase with treads forty-two inches wide, a hand-cut lavatory still present in the master bedroom, and a well in the middle of the floor in the cooking area. All of these features are intact, and your hosts offer tours through this very historic home.

The house was owned and occupied by the Barton family for almost a hundred years, and Dr. Barton practiced medicine in the "office." Since the 1950s there have been three owners of the Barton House, and all have contributed to its restoration and preservation. The original six-room home has been expanded to eighteen rooms, all beautifully furnished in antiques.

Surrounding this historic home are four quaint outbuildings that add to the charm of the grounds. One is the original log cabin of Robert's ancestors, which was carefully restored and moved here. Another is an eighteenth-century cabin that looks historic but was built in 1974 as an antique store. Now, still filled with antiques, it is a delightful one-bedroom-and-bath B&B. Guest Quarters 1 sleeps three guests, and its rough walls, bare floors, and cottage curtains make you feel that it has been on the grounds as long as Barton House itself.

Guest Quarters 2 was built in 1871 as the office of a Dr. Smith at Reed's Lake, Texas (twenty miles east of Salado), and it was moved to this site by the Denmans in 1982 and restored. This ancient cabin sleeps two with its twin beds. Here, too, walls are rough-cut, floors are bare, and antiques fill the room.

Another great feature of Guest Quarters 1 and 2 is that you don't have to browse through the other antique stores. You can just buy everything you see and share in both Guest Quarters.

Barton House and its Guest Quarters sit far off the main street of Salado, but the stone marker awarded in the Texas Centennial attracts visitors who just want to see the house. Fortunately, the Denmans love showing off their beautiful home, so tours are easily available.

Robert and Doris Denman,
innkeepers
Main St.
Salado 76571
(817) 947-5718
2 bedrooms, 2 baths
Moderate
No smoking. No children under
12. No pets.
Deposit required

TYLER HOUSE

*S*alado has a magnificent array of old homes lining its few quiet streets, but one of the oldest is a lovely Greek Revival mansion built by slave labor in 1857. It was first the home of John Flint, an early settler of Salado, but Flint sold the home to Orville Thomas Tyler, one of the eight original Bell County colonists.

Tyler moved his family to Salado in 1864 and became a founding father of Salado College, as well as a county judge and the first, last, and only mayor of Salado. Orville's son, George, continued to live in the mansion and was a prominent figure in Texas politics, too.

The original house was a square two-story structure with chimneys at each end. Additions were made in the late 1930s and in 1971. However, many interesting details of the original house have been preserved. The lamp hooks from which oil lamps hung during the days before electricity are still in the ceilings of each room. Even the old quilting hooks that supported a pulley system for the large quilting frame are intact.

Today you can dine on continental cuisine at its finest, as five of the original rooms are now Barbara's gourmet restaurant. In the formal dining room is a gorgeous walnut canopy, which was the top section of a private box from a Spanish opera house and dates from the nineteenth century. The antique sideboard in the parlor once belonged to Sam Houston. Crafted of walnut with inlaid marble, it was given to a slave, who in turn gave it to the next family who employed her, the Lipscombs. Barbara is a sixth-generation descendant of the Lipscomb family.

Barbara is a fantastic cook and studied under great chefs as well as attending LaVarenne cooking school in Paris. She oversees the preparation of everything served at Tyler House, and many of the specialty dishes on the menu are her own creations. Particularly heavenly are the Bushes Normandy—puff pastries filled with scallops, shrimp, and mushrooms in a delicate cream sauce. You run out of superlatives when you describe this chef's desserts. The new addition to the house is now a very popular piano bar and an intimate spot for Salado's lazy evenings.

Upstairs, Barbara has turned the living quarters into two beautiful suites. The Dalby Suite has a large sitting room with a fireplace, television set, and phone. A handsome antique desk is against one wall, and comfortable blue wingback chairs face the fireplace. There is a huge bath, and the lovely bedroom is papered in an English countryside pattern of teal blue. A thick down comforter in this same pretty blue covers the double bed.

Blue is the basic color in both suites, and the Tyler Suite has a blue tile bath and blue carpet throughout. With its double brass bed and shutters and antique pieces, this suite is equally lovely, even though it does not have a separate parlor. Breakfast is served in the foyer with fresh fruit, juice, and pastries with your morning coffee.

At Tyler House you have all the charm of a historic building, a gourmet restaurant, a fine piano bar, and yet the rural appeal of a small easygoing town. What more could you ask?

Barbara Dalby, innkeeper
Main St.
Salado 76571
(817) 947-5157
2 suites
Exclusive
Mature children only. No pets.

San Antonio

*T*he world's favorite city in Texas needs no introduction. It was founded as San Antonio de Bexar Presidio by Martín de Alarcón on May 3, 1718, as a defense against French encroachment. Prior to the establishment of the missions, Spain considered Texas a no-man's land and unworthy of its time and effort. When the French menace no longer existed and the East Texas missions were abandoned, Bexar remained to become the most famous town in Texas.

BED & BREAKFAST HOSTS
OF SAN ANTONIO

*T*he vivacious organizer of San Antonio's B&Bs got the idea for her project when she was planning a family vacation in New York. Laverne began to worry about the expensive New York hotels and began poring over a guidebook looking for budget hotels. A line that caught her eye read, "Something new in N.Y. for $125 a day." She contacted the agent and was placed in a marvelous centrally located apartment that was perfect for her large group. After a wonderful visit and great lodging at a super price, her son asked her, "Mom, why don't you do this in San Antonio?"

Laverne's B&B business wasn't accomplished quite that easily, but a trip to Fredericksburg cinched her new vocation. She saw Kenn Knopp's B&B sign and went in to see how things were done in that tourist town. Kenn was delighted to show her the ways and means to become Mrs. B&B of San Antonio, and even though Laverne says she wants to keep her business small and friendly, she may have to settle for big and friendly.

Laverne Campbell, director
166 Rockhill
San Antonio 78209
(512) 824-8036

NO. 1

*T*he most frequent request that B&B tourists to the Alamo City make is to stay in the historic King William district. Not only is this old section of the city near downtown, but it is truly hallowed ground. It was originally part of the Alamo's farmland. Many years later, when Ernst Altgelt was naming the streets, he named the main thoroughfare after Wilhelm I, king of Prussia. Anglicized, the entire area became the King William district. Most of the mansions are turn-of-the-century vintage, and many still need a loving hand that owns a fat pocketbook. Most of these ancient homes, however, have been restored, and real estate is quite costly.

One of Laverne's most popular B&B homes is a Victorian masterpiece. Your hostess is a dynamic lady who is involved in all sorts of San Antonio and King William projects. She knows everything about her city and neighborhood, so you will get a real insight into San Antonio. In addition to her community involvement, this tireless dynamo works full time and yet will prepare an authentic Mexican dinner for guests with just a little advance notice.

Your room has twin beds, a small refrigerator, and a private bath. Breakfast is in the vast remodeled kitchen. Your hosts take you right into their family with such warmth and charm that you feel at home immediately. Someone will even pick you up at the airport if necessary.

When you sign the guest register, you will share the pages with the Dutch ambassador to Pakistan and the mayor of Martinique. Even VIPs prefer a B&B's hospitality over an anonymous hotel.

2 bedrooms, 1 bath
Moderate
No small children. No pets.

NO. 2

*I*n the heart of the King William district is a huge, twenty-five-room restored treasure that offers a special apartment for B&B guests. The home is so large that it has three formal parlors and a massive formal dining room. Rich red velvet drapes over lace curtains, handsome antiques, and a gorgeous chandelier are set off with gleaming natural woodwork. Alma, your energetic and charming hostess, said that eight coats of hideous paint had to be removed to restore the beauty of the wood.

Victorians loved gingerbread trim inside their homes as well as on every outside eave and gable. An excellent example of this trend is the wide archway between the parlor and the dining room. Wooden beads and baubles hang in heavy profusion and give a unique flair to the authentic decor.

The guest apartment is absolutely charming, and it is located in the rear of the mansion with its own private entrance. The spacious combination living room—bedroom has a working fireplace and gleaming floors with handsome rugs. In keeping with the Victorian decor, the bath has a claw-foot tub, but a modern shower stall has been added. The sofa makes into a comfortable double bed, and you have an old-fashioned kitchen with a tiny dinette of your own.

The entire yard is surrounded by a high cyclone fence. Nuns lived in this house for a number of years, so the original rock fence was knocked down and the present eight-foot utilitarian wire mesh installed. It seems that every nunnery is required to have an eight-foot fence.

Alma tells the story of a special honeymoon couple who arrived with pink streamers all over their car. After their departure the next day, Alma found bird seed all over the room. She discovered that instead of the traditional rice being thrown at the happy couple, the trend now is to toss bird seed. These newlyweds were special, as both were in their seventies.

1 bedroom, 1 bath
Moderate
No smoking. No small children.
No pets

NO. 3

*N*ot all of the houses in the King William district are in the mansion category. A few "cottages" are snuggled in among the old oaks lining these historic streets. A one-story charmer has been lovingly restored by its owner, who has paid a great deal of attention to detail. Alan did much of the work himself, and he is delighted to show off his Victorian version of a bachelor pad.

Alan's house isn't large enough for a B&B, so he turned the outbuilding in the rear into his guest quarters. You can squeeze in eight people if you're all very friendly, as a group did for a family reunion.

The building is old, and Alan managed to salvage a door, but that's about all. Inside the B&B, walls are modern light pressed-wood paneling, and the full kitchen is brand-new as well. The only antiques are two twin iron beds in the loft that your host found being used as a garden fence. The downstairs bedroom has a double bed with private bath, and the couch makes into a double bed as well. There is even a television, as well as a telephone, in this up-to-date bungalow. Breakfast consists of pastries and juice, and a swing under a Victorian arbor makes an ideal spot in which to sip your morning coffee.

Even though this B&B is today's vintage, Alan will be delighted to give you a tour through his cottage. You can also catch the famous San Antonio dime trolley right at the back door and cruise the entire historic district.

2 bedrooms, 1 bath
Moderate
No smoking. No pets.

NO. 4
RISCHE HOUSE

*I*n the shadow of the medieval Pioneer Flour castle that hovers majestically over the King William district is a small two-story Victorian house that has been transformed into a welcome addition to San Antonio's B&Bs. Even though Rische House is a member of Laverne's organization, they will also take reservations themselves.

A private outside stairway takes you up to another wonderful King William hideaway. Two bedrooms are connected by the bath, which has an old claw-foot tub and pedestal lavatory but no shower. In the front bedroom, the tall windows are level with the floor, which really wasn't unusual in old houses. (They afforded maximum ventilation during hot summer months.)

The back bedroom has twin beds and a closed-in porch. The porch awaits the decorator's touch, however, and it will probably be a "dormitory" for large parties. Furnishings are all antiques that fit the era of the house.

A full kitchen has that wonderful modern invention, the microwave oven, and your hostess serves savory *pan dulces* (sweet rolls) from Mi Tierra Bakery.

It is enchanting to find such unique B&Bs in the King William district. No wonder this is the part of San Antonio that many tourists request.

210 E. Rische
San Antonio 78204
(512) 227-1190
2 bedrooms, 1 bath
Moderate
No smoking. No children under
14. No pets.

NO. 5

*T*he Leon Valley area of San An-tonio is absolutely mushrooming with new subdivisions, yet residents have easy access to the Medical Center and the interstates. Roy and Muriel, like so many of San Antonio's citizens, are retired military personnel. They de-cided that a B&B would be a good idea for them when Roy read an article in the *Wall Street Journal* touting the advantages of becoming a B&B host. They weren't exactly certain how to go about it, but when they heard of Laverne's organization, they were anxious to join.

You can't miss their house when you drive down their street, which is lined with large new homes. Old Glory proudly waves from the front door. This friendly couple has excellent taste in Persian rugs, and the floors and walls of their home reflect their interest and knowledge about this beautiful art. One particularly fine rug hangs over the fireplace and makes a great conversation piece.

The large master bedroom has a Roman bath with sunken tub. If you like, your hosts will make this your guest room, or you can choose between two others that share a bath. One bedroom is bright and cheery, with a double bed that sports a yellow and orange flowered spread; the other is cool and comfortable in shades of light blue.

You will be treated to a full breakfast, and Roy and Muriel have no objections to smokers or older children.

2 bedrooms, 1 bath
Moderate
No pets

NO. 6

*N*ot far from Brackenridge Park is a funky old neighborhood built during the 1920s. Every city has this type of area, with small clapboard houses and almost every room on a small scale. The living rooms are tiny, with tiny fireplaces. Two little bedrooms share a teensy bath with a claw-foot tub and no shower. There was never any room in the kitchen for a dinette, so the dining room was used for every meal. One has the feeling that some vast mail-order house made a fortune off this basic floor plan, for this house was no doubt once the America dream of the middle class. Now this same little house is extremely popular with singles, and many of these vintage cottages are being restored and remodeled into marvelous, fashionable homes.

The hostess of this B&B is a vivacious lady who has furnished her clapboard residence in keeping with its era. Armoires, a parlor set, lots of antique knickknacks, an upright piano of some bygone year, and even a gas stove all look like they came with the house. A massive Eastlake Victorian double bed dominates the small bedroom, but an adjoining porch has been converted into a closet. Breakfast is continental and served in the dining room.

This darling house has a lot of charm and is certainly a reflection of its owner's intelligence, good taste, and delightful wit.

1 bedroom, 1 bath
Moderate
No smoking. No children.
No pets

NO. 7

*E*very new subdivision has its multitude of garden homes, and northwest San Antonio has its share as well. One particularly lovely garden home in this area has become a very popular B&B, perhaps because of its location, its charming decor, and its entertaining hostess.

Susan's favorite color is no doubt salmon, for throughout her house this is the predominant color. Throw pillows, chairs, bedspread, bath, and wallpaper are highlighted with this restful shade. The entire house is beautifully decorated with comfortable modern furniture, and you can snuggle on a big sofa before a small fire, sip a glass of wine, and listen to the soft stereo for a perfect romantic evening. The guest room with its double bed is equally well appointed and nice.

A redwood deck with chaise lounges is piled high with potted plants, and you can easily surmise that gardening on a small scale is Susan's favorite hobby.

You will have this comfort to yourself, as Susan is a working gal and works nights. She does arrive back home in time for your breakfast; as your day begins, Susan's ends.

2 bedrooms, 1 bath
Moderate
No smoking. No children.
No pets

*I*n the Leon Valley area of the Alamo City, a professor of psychology and his entertaining wife provide their guests with the ultimate in sleeping comfort: a king-sized waterbed. This spacious downstairs bedroom has a private bath, telephone, and television, and it is a favorite with business travelers. An Indian-motif bedspread adds warmth to the bedroom's decor.

Out in the shady backyard a German Shepherd with a floppy ear pants an invitation to come out and share his domain. A swing rocks gently to and fro, waiting for you to take Jasmine up on her pleas.

One of the loveliest features of this B&B is Pat's fantastic collection of Lladro porcelain. Every room has a special nook and shelves for these exquisite pieces. You can spend hours just admiring these delicate figurines and listening to Pat's tales about each acquisition.

If you inquire of your hosts about a good place to dine, you may find yourself at the best meal in town without ever having to get in your car. Many B&B hosts like their guests so much that they invite them to dinner. This is just another of the many reasons that B&Bs are gaining such widespread popularity throughout Texas.

1 bedroom, 1 bath
Moderate
No smoking. No small children.
No pets

NO. 9

*B*ack in 1691, Texas's most popu-
lar town was called Yanaguana. Fortunately, Fray Damian Massanet changed
it to San Antonio de Padua, then to become San Antonio de Bexar. Eventually this area became Alamo Heights, and despite San Antonio's schemes
to annex it, the subdivision was voted an independent municipality in 1922.
So in this historic part of the city, Alamo Heights is still a favorite place to
live, and a great location for a B&B.

A great deal of the charm of a B&B is that each is different, and you are
really never totally prepared for what will be waiting for you. It's that little
element of surprise that makes staying in a B&B exciting. A real gem in
Alamo Heights is a Cape Cod guest house complete with antiques. The only
thing missing is the Atlantic Ocean, or you would swear you were in New
England. Instead, you are near the McNay Art Museum in San Antonio.

This wonderful guest house is perfect for a night or a year. If you visit in
the winter, a tile-front fireplace casts its glow over the sitting room. A queen-
sized four-poster canopied bed dominates the bedroom, and a full kitchen
and small bath complete this excellent B&B. On the bar of the kitchen, a
basket of breakfast treats awaits you, to be sampled whenever you wish.

In addition to all this luxury, a redwood deck stretches out through the
trees of the backyard. It seems as if you have your very own treehouse right
in the middle of nowhere, instead in the middle of a bustling city.

If you love elegant music and yearn to render your own versions of Chopin
or Mozart, your hostess, Nancy, will insist that you enjoy her grand piano in
the music room of the main house. She will also offer country club privileges.
What heaven!

1 bedroom, 1 bath
Exclusive
No smoking. No children.
No pets

NO. 10

*A*t this northeast San Antonio B&B you get full service. Not only will your hosts pick you up at the airport, but they will also take you places to see in a city that has more than its share of tourist attractions. Talk about a red-carpet welcome! Roger and Alice are at your service. They will also accept well-behaved children.

Actually, the accommodations in this typical suburban home are perfect for families. Two of the three bedrooms have twin beds, and all three share a bath. Children and adults alike will be enchanted with the doll collection, as well as an old-fashioned button collection. According to Alice's legend, when girls have saved a thousand buttons, they will meet their future husbands.

The double bed is an antique spool bed with pink and white coverlets. Walls are painted, and several are hung with specially designed quilts that belonged to Alice's mother. Quilted throw pillows add to the warmth of the room. One of the twin beds is a lovely antique piece with rounded head- and footboards. A screened porch looks over a tidy yard that slopes down to a small creek, giving a touch of country to a B&B in the heart of a major city.

This retired Air Force officer and his wife, a former librarian, still travel extensively and continue to add interesting mementos of their journeys to their home.

3 bedrooms, 1 bath
Moderate
No smoking. No pets.

NO. 11

*J*ust a hop, skip, and jump from San Antonio's famous medical complex is a very nice Spanish-style home that offers a delightful B&B. When you ring the bell, don't let that huge Doberman frighten you away; once you're inside, Baron turns into a big lap dog, and he is totally harmless.

Alice, your hostess, is a court reporter, sings solo in the church choir, and will arrange a bridge game for you. This kind, generous lady also picks you up at the airport and doesn't object to either very young or teenage children. In fact, she had a young man who was alone to pick up his adopted baby and received the baby before he had all the official papers completed. Alice helped care for the infant and even fixed a bed in a dresser drawer until the young father could return home.

The living room and guest room are filled with lovely porcelain collectibles, and most of them were Alice's mother's. They give a very personal touch to the home and make you feel welcome. One other bedroom is done in tones of light blue and has a queen-sized bed.

Breakfast is served in the small dining area, with its strawberry draperies, placemats, and cream and sugar set. If you do have to spend time at the nearby Medical Center, you couldn't ask for a cheerier place to come back to. The B&B is also within easy driving distance of downtown, for the freeway is just a few blocks away.

**Contact Bed & Breakfast Texas
Style
4224 W. Red Bird Ln.
Dallas 75237
(214) 298-8586
1 bedroom, 1 bath
Moderate
No smoking. No pets.**

San Antonio Number 11

INTERNATIONAL HOSTEL AND GUEST HOUSE

*D*uring the Indian Wars of the late 1800s, the United States Cavalry stationed in the Trans-Pecos relied heavily on their Seminole Indian scouts to find the elusive Comanches and Apaches. These brilliant trackers were of mixed Indian and Negro blood and had been ousted from Florida. Their bravery became legend, and three were winners of the Medal of Honor. After the frontier was settled, many of the scouts remained in Del Rio, and their descendants are still contributing to the area's heritage.

In command of these phenomenal scouts was John Lapham Bullis. From 1873 to 1881 Bullis was cited four times for gallant service. After the Indian Wars, Bullis was promoted to major and made paymaster at Fort Sam Houston. In 1905 President Roosevelt appointed him brigadier general, and Bullis retired the same year.

In 1909 Bullis built a neoclassical-style mansion just across from Fort Sam Houston. Designed by noted architect Harvey Page with large Greek columns surrounding the wide porch, the mansion's elegance has been preserved inside and out. Ornate designs and fine chandeliers enhance the fourteen-foot ceilings. Floors are inlaid with geometric patterns of rare woods, and the massive staircase with its forty-four steps is carved from oak. All of the fireplaces are of beautiful marble.

While Bullis House is not exactly your standard B&B, it deserves recognition, for it is now one of the few youth hostels in this part of the Southwest. When you think of hosteling, you think of being young, sleeping in a dormitory, meeting people from different countries, and having an inexpensive, safe night's lodging. Well, Bullis House is all of those things, but it also has a lovely room with a double bed and private bath on the first floor and other double and single rooms that share a bath upstairs. All come with continental breakfast. There is also a reading room with television, a small kitchen for guests to use, and picnic tables on the grounds.

While most of the guests are foreigners, American travelers are often here as well. Rates are low for the hostel ($6.25 for American Youth Hostel members), and sheets and towels are available for rent. There are more individual rooms that could be adapted to B&B, but each now accommodates ten people.

If you do want to stay in a gorgeous mansion at real bargain prices, Bullis House is the answer.

Alma and Steve Cross, managers
621 Pierce
P. O. Box 8059
San Antonio 78208
(512) 223-9426
1 bedroom, 1 bath
2 dormitories, 2 baths
Budget
No pets

Crystal River Inn

San Marcos

CRYSTAL RIVER INN

*T*he old town of San Marcos took its name from the river that runs through it, which the Spanish christened for Saint Mark. And as a major post on the Camino Real, famous and infamous figures in Texas history passed this way. People still pass through San Marcos, but these days mostly to stop and play at the fabulous Aquarena Springs. San Marcos is a lovely setting for the Crystal River Inn.

Near the turn of the century, William Daniel Wood of Indiana arrived in San Marcos to become an editor, a leading attorney, a member of the state legislature, and finally a judge. Befitting his status, Wood built a victorian mansion in the best part of town. As often happens with old neighborhoods, this stretch of Hopkins Street became commercial, with only a few original homes remaining. Now, thanks to the Dillons, who invested lots of work and lots of love, Judge Wood's mansion has been beautifully restored. He would feel right at home in the Crystal River Inn.

The Dillons are avid river rats, and the name of their inn sets the tone for the decor: four gorgeous bedrooms have been christened for Texas Hill Country streams. Downstairs, the Frio room is a cool ice blue, with matching wallpaper and draperies. A snow-white comforter on the double bed accentuates the cool theme that Frio implies. The Frio shares a bath with the Pedernales. In the Pedernales room, the ornate antique double bed's canopy is dark blue with bright pink peonies. Both the Frio and the Pedernales have small, working fireplaces and wicker seating areas.

Upstairs, the honeymoon suite is named for the Medina. With its queen-sized bed and cozy fireplace, this is a room for lovers. A white-on-white bedspread and antique satin draperies lend a special elegance to this beautiful room.

Also upstairs is the Colorado room. As you would think, desert tones of soft beige and brown characterize this room. Indian rugs add a bright splash of color, and the queen-sized bed is canopied in a most unusual rope design.

The huge kitchen and dining area are located behind the friendly, handsome parlor. Blue and white tiles frame the windows and work area, and you can see this is Cathy's kingdom. Here she prepares fresh fruit, beer bisquits, and plump sausages for breakfast. In good weather, breakfast is served on a beautiful little patio.

Crystal River Inn is perfectly located for visiting the attractions of either San Antonio or Austin.

Cathy and Mike Dillon,
innkeepers
Crystal River Inn
326 W. Hopkins
San Marcos 78666
(512) 396-3739
4 bedrooms. 3 baths
Moderate
No restrictions on children or
smokers

Seguin

LAKE PLACID GUEST HOUSE

*O*ne of the best-kept Guadalupe River secrets is Seguin. The very same river that makes New Braunfels so popular flows through Seguin. While there may not be rapids or white water, the river is just as refreshing and beautiful as it is farther up. No only that, but Seguin is a fine old Texas town with a handsome square that boasts the world's largest pecan tree. Now Seguin can also boast of having one of Texas's best B&Bs.

This charming riverfront cottage doesn't seem all that impressive from the front, but when you go inside and see that beautiful view of the Guadalupe through huge windows on the rear, you know that you have found an idyllic retreat. There is a porch of your very own, or you can go down to the patio and swing in contentment as the river drifts slowly by. Lake Placid is a very appropriate name for this special area of the Guadalupe.

Your hostess used to be a commercial artist, and her brochures are just delightful. She has furnished the guest house in French Provincial pieces, which adds a touch of elegance. This cottage formerly belonged to a corporation executive and will sleep six. It has a full kitchen, but Joyce fixes breakfast in her house at your convenience. There are fishing and boating docks, and Lake Placid is ideal for water skiing. Joyce will even take you on a partyboat trip or make a paddleboat available. This lady offers the epitome of riverfront hospitality—even television.

You simply must get your family or friends together and enjoy the Lake Placid Guest House at least once a year, no matter what season you choose. It's only thirty minutes from San Antonio off Interstate Highway 10.

Joyce Lawrence, hostess
945 Reiley Rd.
Seguin 78155
(512) 379-7830
2 bedrooms, 1 bath
Moderate
Dangerous for small children
No pets

Temple

*L*ong before Interstate Highway 35 bisected Temple, the Gulf, Colorado, the Santa Fe Railroad decided that it was an important stop on an important route. When the town was established in 1880, the railroad executives decided to name it for their chief construction engineer, B. M. Temple. Today most people think of Temple in connection with one of the Southwest's leading medical centers, Scott-White Hospital and Clinic. While Temple is not exactly a tourist town, visitors do come from all over the world to its outstanding medical facilities.

*I*n a quiet, modern residential section of this old railroad town just a few blocks from the interstate is a brick home with a Pennsylvania "Wilkom" sign on its door. You will be glad you came, for Earl and Yvonne have a delightful B&B with two bedrooms, each with double beds. Earl is a research scientist, and both he and Yvonne are eager to share ideas with their guests.

A major treat of this B&B is a large landscaped swimming pool, shaded by a magnificent purple crape myrtle tree. A continental breakfast is served in a tiny yellow gazebo by the pool.

Temple is an excellent point from which to tour Central Texas, and this B&B makes a great headquarters.

**Contact Bed & Breakfast Texas
Style
4224 W. Red Bird Ln.
Dallas 75237
(214) 298-8586
2 bedrooms, 1 bath
Moderate
No smoking. No pets.**

Wimberley

*W*imberley is the perfect location in which to savor the ambience of the Hill Country and yet be close to San Antonio and Austin. Now a major resort area in Texas, Wimberley is "western cute" with its gift shops and pioneer-town atmosphere. The Wimberley flea market is held on the first Saturday of each month from March to November, with lots of booths for browsing.

BED & BREAKFAST OF WIMBERLEY

*I*f you want some Texas real estate around Wimberley, you might try Larry Laltomus at Lone Man Realty. His A-frame office is on the outskirts of town. Larry sort of fell into B&B when clients needed a place to stay. He fixed up the upstairs of his office into two

147

bedrooms, and his small lobby became a parlor. You have to go downstairs to the bath, but this is an economical B&B.

Larry Laltomus, director
P. O. Box 589
Wimberley 78676
(512) 847-9666
2 bedrooms, 1 bath
Budget
No restrictions

HERITAGE HILL

"*Y*our heaven for a home" is the modest slogan of this most unusual B&B on the Blanco River near Wimberley. Here in the heart of the Hill Country is a splendid Japanese palace set in an exquisite Oriental garden. Your hosts, Sam and Alice, are native Texans. In fact, Alice's ancestor, Adolphus Sterne, was a noted friend of Sam Houston. You might expect them to prefer a Texas pioneer home, but it is the mysterious East that fascinates this interesting couple.

In 1397 the shogun of Japan built a beautiful Golden Pavilion in Kyoto, and the one-room third story of the pavilion was his place of worship. The walls were lined with gold, and the ruler became an ardent Buddhist. When Sam and Alice decided that they wanted an exact replica of this fabulous building, their architect found the complete details in the University of Texas library. The interior of the Texas version of the Golden Pavilion has been altered to accommodate modern conveniences, but the home's proportions are identical to the original.

Inside are priceless Oriental art objects, and Alice has displayed them handsomely. However, the third floor "worship room" is now a functional office and merely lined with gold wallpaper. It is rather disconcerting to sit among all this Oriental splendor and talk Texas history with one of the grande dames of the Daughters of the Republic of Texas!

The setting for this "temple" is around a 300-year-old tree that is used as a centerpiece of the design. A traditional plum tree is planted at each corner of the pavilion, and a Lhasa apso and a Pekinese fit in with the scenario. The silly border collie that plays with rocks is out of Oriental character, but so lovable that it doesn't matter. Wind chimes tinkle merrily on all corners of the three decks, and a romantic "moon-gazing deck" offers a lovely view of the Hill Country even when the sun is shining.

The B&B portion of this incredible little home is a charming teahouse off to the side. Steps lead down to a private swimming hole in the Blanco River, and a hillside secluded patio is perfect for sunbathing. The teahouse guest quarters has all the luxuries you could desire: private bedroom and bath, a full kitchen, a complete stereo radio with tape deck, a fireplace, a grand piano, and last, but certainly not least, a pool table. This is a B&B made for romance, but children are welcome, and there are six extra beds.

Sam and Alice have received many postcards from friends who have seen the real Golden Pavilion in Kyoto, but somehow these two avid proponents of Japanese culture have never been to the Orient at all!

1 bedroom, 1 bath
6 extra beds
Exclusive
No pets

Dallas, Fort Worth, and Northeast Texas

Dallas, Fort Worth and Northeast Texas

BED & BREAKFAST TEXAS STYLE

*M*ost of the B&Bs in this section are listed with Bed & Breakfast Texas Style. By far the largest organization of its kind in the state, this Dallas agency has grown from a handful of host homes in 1982 to around a hundred B&Bs now in cities large and small. And it's still growing. The only statewide bed and breakfast referral service, it has host homes from Austin to Arlington, from Carthage to Colleyville, from Dallas to Denison. Included in its listings are lakeside retreats, ranches, inner-city houses and suburban neighborhoods, modern and Victorian, modest and sumptuous. A few were mentioned in earlier sections of this book.

Featured on television shows such as "Good Morning America" and "CBS Morning News," as well as in major publications like *Texas Highways*, Bed & Breakfast Texas Style is the brainchild of Ruth Wilson of Dallas. The former schoolteacher became intrigued with the concept after reading about it in a newspaper. Since she had always enjoyed entertaining, opening her own home to B&B guests seemed like a natural thing to do. Discovering that a referral service was needed, she organized her own, determined from the start to develop a statewide network. Obviously, she has succeeded.

Ruth points out that most hosts do not open their homes to B&B guests just for the money, but rather for the chance to meet interesting, adventurous people from all walks of life, from this country and abroad. Although the bed and breakfast program is primarily a network for private residences, a few small hotels and inns also belong to Ruth Wilson's organization, such as the Thomas J. Rusk Hotel in Rusk.

All of Ruth Wilson's listings reviewed in this section are in the Dallas area and North and Northeast Texas. Ruth's listings are designated by BBTS and a number. Other B&Bs, such as the Pecan Inn of Clarksville and Casa Cabrito in Flower Mound, are also included in the city listings. The Pecan Inn accepts its own reservations, and Casa Cabrito is listed with Laverne Campbell of San Antonio. In addition, all the B&Bs in Jefferson, the undisputed bed and breakfast capital of Texas, make their own reservations direct.

Ruth Wilson, director
4224 W. Red Bird Ln.
Dallas 75237
(214) 298-8586

Arlington

BBTS NO. 1

*I*t's been said that a man's home is his castle, but in the case of this B&B, *hacienda* would probably be more appropriate. That's because this immense home on the edge of Arlington near east Fort Worth has an undeniable south-of-the-border flavor, from the terra cotta brick exterior to the imported Mexican furniture found throughout.

A prominent Arlington physician and his wife designed their sprawling showstopper themselves inside and out. Since both are native Texans, they wanted their home to reflect the Spanish influence that is so strong in the Southwest, and it does just that. Informal elegance is probably the best way to describe this open, airy B&B, which has a circular driveway in front. Even the foyer makes a dramatic statement, with a 150-year-old trunk, a hand-carved bench, and an antique mirror. When lit, a fluorescent light on the mirror reveals an etching of a Spanish courtyard.

The dining room, living room, and spacious garden room provide a sweeping panorama. A spectacular floor-to-ceiling glass wall draws your eye to the peanut-shaped pool and pond beyond. There is a wrought-iron glass-topped table by the glass wall, which is where breakfast is usually served. Who needs food when you can feast your eyes on the beauty all around?

But breakfast is something special, just like the house itself. Don't be surprised at some exotic dishes you might be served, such as a banana topped with Cool Whip (something the hosts sampled on a recent cruise) or a special crepe embellished with the outline of the state of Texas, deep fried, and dusted with powdered sugar.

The master bedroom is off the garden room, and the four guest rooms are in another wing, so you'll have complete privacy. Each of the four rooms, which belonged to the couple's four daughters, has its own personality. One is pink and white with two bright pink chairs and a double bed. A blue bathroom next to it will be shared with guests in the Bluebonnet Room, which has a circular king-sized wrought-iron headboard. A silk bluebonnet arrangement and a painting and decorative plate carry out the bluebonnet motif. As a B&B memento, you'll receive a package of bluebonnet seeds.

Across the hall is the lilac room, which has a queen-sized bed with a lilac wicker headboard, a built-in vanity, and wicker furniture. Lilac, of course, is the predominant color. This room has its own bath.

The fourth room is a complete contrast, with heavy furniture imported from Mexico like most of that in the house, including the queen-sized bed, a chest, and a mirror. A genuine New Zealand lambskin, a present from missionary friends, is on a wooden rocker. There is a bath next door. Between this room and the lilac room is a telephone on a revolving built-in panel, which parents of teenagers can appreciate.

Despite its elegance, this is a very comfortable home just made for entertaining. Relax before the fireplace or out by the pool or pond. Swim, fish, or jog around the neighborhood. Though the mailing address of this B&B is Arlington, it is actually in Dalworthington Gardens, a small unincorporated town inside Arlington. The host explains that during the depression President Franklin D. Roosevelt gave five acres of land to each person living in that rural area for vegetable gardens. Since this was midway between Dallas and Fort Worth and right next to Arlington, you can see how they arrived at the name Dalworthington Gardens. At that time Arlington was just a sleepy little community, but it eventually grew up around Dalworthington Gardens, which named its main thoroughfare Roosevelt Drive, in honor of the president.

The hosts have lived here for twenty years. The B&B is easily accessible from Interstate Highway 20, and it would make an unforgettable stopover if you have business anywhere in the Metroplex. The Texas Sports Hall of

Fame, Traders Village, Six Flags, Southwestern Historical Wax Museum, and other area attractions beckon, too, if you have time.

4 bedrooms, 3 baths
Moderate
No smoking. No pets.

BBTS NO. 2

*I*f you're a fan of water, you'll be ecstatic with this imposing two-story Arlington home, which is on a cul-de-sac in an exclusive neighborhood. In back is a picturesque canal, and water is visible from every room of this sumptuous French country-style showplace, including the bed and breakfast rooms upstairs. A wide wooden deck goes from one end of the house in back to the other on both the first and second stories. On nice days, you can sit out there and watch the ducks and swans glide by. A weeping willow by the deck adds to the natural beauty.

The hosts have only one room available at a time for bed and breakfast guests, but they alternate among three rooms for this purpose. One has a plum decor and a queen-sized bed; another, done in tones of cream, has an antique brass double bed; and a third has twin beds. Professionally decorated, all three have ceiling fans and doors that open onto the deck. Just specify ahead of time which room best meets your needs. All three rooms are equally lovely, just like the rest of the house, which is the epitome of elegance inside and out.

The dining room has a lead crystal chandelier, a blue hand-tied Oriental rug from India, and Oriental accents. Step down to the left, and you're in a formal living room, exquisitely appointed with a grand piano (play a tune if you wish), hand-carved 184-year-old cranberry chairs, and another beautiful rug from India. It's blue, too.

The spacious family room in the wing at far right has a wet bar and several conversation pieces, including a mounted duck shot by the host, a successful businessman who has an equally successful wife. Her office, one of the smaller downstairs rooms, has floor-to-ceiling shelves filled with books.

Easily reached from Interstate Highway 30, this dazzling home will be an unforgettable retreat, whether you have business in nearby Fort Worth or anyplace else in the Metroplex. It's also very close to area attractions like Six Flags.

1 bedroom, 1 bath
Moderate
No smoking. No pets.

Carthage

BBTS NO. 3

*L*ooking like something you'd see
in a movie, this magnificent two-story New Orleans–style white colonial
home in the East Texas town of Carthage is probably the most impressive
listing with Bed & Breakfast Texas Style. Situated on twenty-six acres of pastureland, encircled by a picturesque white rail fence, the home can't be seen
from the highway. A long tree-studded road leads to the circular driveway in
front of the house, which has a second-floor wrought-iron balcony. With a
huge courtyard across from the parking area in front and a gazebo and pool in
back, the grounds are impressive, too. Although the hostess raised race
horses at one time, only a few horses and four cows roam the pastureland
now. But they give the B&B added appeal. Guests usually get up early just to
wander around the property or perhaps relax in the garden room as the sun
floods the plant-filled atrium and adjoining greenhouse.

Though exquisitely furnished, Dixie's home is very comfortable. As she
points out, after housing four children and entertaining five grandchildren,
her home is "childproof," so well-behaved children are welcome. All the

rooms in the house are very large and decorated in warm yet vibrant colors, including the formal living room.

There are three guest rooms. The downstairs bedroom has a mahogany four-poster double bed with a canopy, brown wicker chairs and a loveseat, and a private bath. At the top of the curved staircase is the Nantucket Room, named for the charming island thirty miles off the coast of Massachusetts, where Dixie loves to vacation. Blue quilted covers on the twin beds complement the distinctive blue and white woven Dhurrie rug and coordinated wallpaper. French doors lead to the second-floor balcony that overlooks the courtyard, where the family has frequently entertained and held dances through the years. The third room has two single beds with a wicker love seat and antique butternut chairs similar to ones in the Lincoln Bedroom in the White House. An antique armoire is also in the feminine-looking room, which has a good view of the beautiful backyard. The latter two rooms also have private baths.

Dixie, who loves to travel, garden, and play bridge, fixes a bountiful breakfast for B&B guests, who can eat in the gazebo by the pool, on the screened-in porch by the den, in the sunny garden room (which has green and yellow cushions on the white wicker furniture), or anyplace else in the luxurious home. The gracious hostess places a basket of fresh fruit and chocolate mints in the guest rooms at night as an added personal touch. You'll experience southern hospitality at its best in this Carthage home.

Staying at this very special B&B is in itself worth a trip, but it is also in an ideal location if you are planning a trek to Jefferson (bed and breakfast homes there are often filled up on weekends) or to the races at Louisiana Downs, both about forty miles away. Consider an overnight stay here, too, if you are attending the famed Rose Festival in nearby Tyler. Carthage has its own festival, Potlatch, which you might also want to take in. (Miss Texas, who has appeared at this arts and crafts festival for the past few years, has been Dixie's house guest.)

Besides being the county seat of Panola County, Carthage is the home of the legendary country-western singer, Jim Reeves, who died in a plane crash in 1964. A life-sized statue of Reeves is one of the small town's attractions. Dixie will be glad to provide directions to the statue, to nearby Lake Murvail, which has excellent recreational facilities, or even to a local restaurant that has been attracting fans from near and far for more than forty years because of its hearty country fare like chicken-fried steak.

3 bedrooms, 3 baths
Exclusive
No smoking. No pets.

Clarksville

PECAN INN

*P*ecan trees tower over this charming turn-of-the-century Clarksville home, which has four well-appointed rooms open to bed and breakfast guests. So it seems appropriate that Pecan Inn was the name chosen by the new owners for what had long been known as the old Wooley homeplace when they acquired it in the fall of 1984.

Built between 1846 and 1860—records pinpointing the date have disappeared—Pecan Inn is an eleven-room, two-story frame house with six fireplaces, windows that go almost from the floor to the ceiling, a spiral staircase, period furnishings of impeccable taste, and a modern touch, airconditioning. The spacious 6,000-square-foot jewel also has a parlor filled with an extensive library, games, and a television. A sun room has been converted to a dining room, and there are nice antiques on both floors. (A full-course meal with wine is available for $6.50 nightly to B&B guests only.) Wayne and Johanna Fowler, the inkeepers, have had long careers in the music business, and they have displayed gold records of Elvis Presley, Dolly Parton, and other famous singers whom they've helped promote.

You'll experience the graciousness of times gone by in this out-of-the-way inn. The warm hospitality extended by the hosts include a complimentary cheese and cracker tray and fresh lemonade upon arrival, and homemade pie—pecan, of course—that evening. A full southern breakfast, complete with homemade preserves, will be served in the sun room.

Three of the guest rooms are named after former owners. The A. J. Martin Bluebonnet Room downstairs has a queen-sized white wicker bed, a rose carpet, navy and rose paper, and a bluebonnet painting over the fireplace. Martin's granddaughter, whose last name was Wooley, inherited the house, which she kept until 1960. It had been in the family for more than sixty years.

At the top of the spiral staircase is the George F. Lawton Poppy Room, which has a dark maple four-poster bed. Other attention-getters are an antique washstand and dresser. A poppy painting over the mantel blends beautifully with the gold wallpaper. Lawton, by the way, was the original owner.

The second upstairs bedroom, the John W. O'Neill Daisy Room, not surprisingly has a painting of daisies above the mantel, along with an old oak high headboard double bed and a birds-eye maple wardrobe. Both the poppy and daisy rooms have claw-foot tubs beside the beds. A former owner converted the tiny closets to accommodate commodes and lavatories.

You can hike, bike, or ride horseback around the tree-studded grounds (which cover seven acres), play croquet, fish on the lake in back, or just relax in the front-porch swing. If time permits, visit Clarksville's courthouse, third oldest in the state, or take advantage of the nearby city lake.

Located just off Highway 37 north on Old Albion Rd., Pecan Inn is hard to miss, especially in the summer when the Texas, Confederate, and American flags are flapping in the Northeast Texas breeze. Since there is only one motel in town, Pecan Inn has become popular with families and friends visiting Clarksville natives, as well as those with business in the small town, which is only twenty-three miles from the Oklahoma border and not far from Texarkana or Sherman. The Pecan Inn is helping put Clarksville on the map!

Old Albion Rd.
Clarksville 75426
(214) 427-5507
4 bedrooms, 4 baths (1 shared)
Moderate
Smoking outside only
Discounts for three days or more

Pecan Inn

Clifton

BBTS NO. 4

*I*f you yearn for country air and open spaces and a more relaxed pace, this comfortable Clifton farmhouse is for you. You'll forget your cares on this sprawling hilltop retreat, which is about forty miles from Waco. Besides, your children will have a ball with the cows and kittens, guineas and geese. You'll even see plenty of wild rabbits if you walk down the country road behind the house. The nearest neighbor is about a quarter of a mile away.

This has been the family home of the hostess for more than twenty-five years. One room is her office. Vivian is a free-lance architectural designer who loves exchanging ideas and philosophies with her guests. She has two guest rooms, one with a private bath, the other shared; both have double beds. Guests are welcome to watch television in the den, which has a wood-burning stove. The country air ought to give you a good appetite for a hearty breakfast of sausage and scrambled eggs, which can be eaten on the patio during warm months. For an extra fee, Vivian will fix other meals, since there aren't many places to eat in Clifton.

If she has time, Vivian will also conduct sightseeing excursions to the nearby Texas Safari Wildlife Park. A retired Baylor University mascot—a bear, of course—is a resident there. Lake Whitney is only ten miles away, and Vivian knows some excellent fishing guides. The Bosque Memorial Museum in Clifton might be of interest, too, but it's open only on weekends.

2 bedrooms
2 baths (1 shared)
Budget
No restrictions

Colleyville

BBTS NO. 5

*T*his is a peach of a place. In fact, there are peach trees on the three acres surrounding this luxurious contemporary home in an exclusive Colleyville neighborhood. And when the trees are laden with fruit, overnight guests will have peaches for breakfast, along with blueberry muffins or croissants, coffee, and juice. Irene rolls in a cart so guests can have breakfast in bed.

One guest bedroom has a queen-sized bed, a chaise lounge, a wicker trunk, and a small television set. A large red Oriental fan is the focal point in the second room, which has twin beds. Both rooms have ceiling fans and private baths, not to mention a lot of charm.

Though Colleyville isn't as well known as some cities with bed and breakfast homes, it is in a great location, only a half hour from either Fort Worth or Dallas and fifteen minutes from DFW Airport. It's a ranch country retreat, and you'll drive by longhorn steers and horses to reach this well-appointed brick home. The hosts themselves have some beautiful big bulls that formerly roamed Texas's famed King Ranch, as well as a golden retriever, a self-appointed member of the welcoming committee.

Take time for a swim in the heated rectangular-shaped pool or go for a walk and enjoy the country air. There is a creek with a bridge on the gently rolling grounds. The congenial hosts, retired airline people from the East who still travel extensively, will enjoy showing you their greenhouse and tomato plants, too.

2 bedrooms, 2 baths
Moderate
No smoking. No children. No
pets.

Dallas

W here else but in Big D can you
find horse stables almost within the shadow of a gleaming gold skyscraper?
Characterized by casual sophistication, endless cultural opportunities, and a
healthy business climate, Dallas has evolved into the nation's seventh largest
city. An important center of fashion, banking, and of course oil interests,
Dallas is drawing an increasing number of business and vacation visitors
from abroad, as well as from closer destinations.

Whether you come to Dallas for business or for pleasure, take time to explore the city. Downtown Dallas has Thanksgiving Square (a spectacular in-
terfaith chapel with a number of exhibits), the new Sculpture Garden, the
restored Majestic Theatre, the West End Historical District, and much more.
The visitors' center at Union Station can provide directions.

Old City Park is another must if you have time. Located near downtown,
the restored turn-of-the-century village features crafts synonymous with that
era and pottery made in the park in the McCall's Museum gift shop. You can
pick up unusual mementos in the store, such as handmade walnut dominoes
inlaid with spruce, lye soap, or a Texian Campaign plate that took seven

years to reproduce accurately. Try the restored Brent Place Restaurant for a country-style lunch.

The Biblical Arts Center near NorthPark Shopping Center might well prove to be a highlight of your stay in Dallas. A massive mural, taller than a two-story house and almost half as long as a football field, depicts the miracle at Pentecost, one of the most dramatic events of the early Christian era. The giant wall painting is enhanced by special lighting, narration, and stereo music.

Fair Park, with its many excellent museums, can keep you spellbound, too, and not just during the State Fair, which is held each fall. First-rate musicals are offered at Fair Park during the fall and summer months.

Plan to gain a few pounds in Dallas, because the city has countless top-quality budget-breaking restaurants such as the Adolphus's French Room, the famed Pyramid Room at the Fairmont, Il Sorrento, Jean Claude's, Mario's, and the Mansion at Turtle Creek. If you yearn for country cooking and more economical prices, Dallas has those, too, along with a wide variety of ethnic eateries. (Your B&B hosts can steer you in the right direction.)

With all the caloric temptations, overindulging isn't hard to do, but you can work off excess calories and perhaps even executive stress by jogging at White Rock Lake in East Dallas or Bachman Lake (Northwest Highway and Bachman). You can also jog at the spectacular new Downtown YMCA, 601 N. Akard, which has a $10 guest fee for nonmembers. Or exercise in style at the world-famous Aerobic Center for a nominal guest tab. Located on twenty-eight wooded acres at 12100 Preston Road, facilities include the famous Cooper Clinic.

If you have time, treat yourself to a steak or barbecue dinner at Texas Lil's Diamond A Ranch at Justin, a 200-acre spread about forty-five minutes from Dallas. The dude ranch has a covered picnic pavilion, horseback riding, hayrides, and an Olympic-sized pool. Now this is Texas, podner!

Dallas has one of the few remaining custom-boot craftsmen, by the way. Ramirez Boot Shop in Oak Cliff can personalize custom boots with initials, a map of Texas, a replica of an oil well, or even a Dallas Cowboy helmet.

If you're wondering about that horse stable, it's on Park Lane, a block east of Central Expressway. Dallas is a city of surprises. Discover it for yourself, and enhance your visit by enjoying the hospitality of one of the many area bed and breakfast homes.

BBTS NO. 6 (DOWNTOWN)

*H*ere is a chic townhouse within the shadow of the skyscrapers of downtown Dallas. The B&B hostess is one of a growing number of professionals who live in Bryan Place, a small new inner-city neighborhood planned as an experiment by one of the nation's largest home builders, Fox and Jacobs, in 1979. After removing some buildings and bulldozing other old ones in the area, they created a very attractive community of single-family homes and condominiums. Victorian touches, narrow cobblestone streets, postage-stamp yards, and old-fashioned street lamps have made Bryan Place most inviting.

Named for John Neely Bryan, the founder of Dallas, the subdivision has homes and townhouses that are not only near town, but also offer opportunities for exploration and adventure. The spectacular new Dallas Museum of Art, the Majestic Theatre, Deep Ellum (an arts district), and the West End Historical District are minutes away. Lower Greenville Avenue, with attractions like the Grenada Theater, which features cult and foreign films, and Oak Lawn are other areas you might want to explore if you stay at this novel B&B.

Since the hostess grew up in Flushing Meadows, Queens, her affinity for an inner-city neighborhood is perhaps understandable. Maria is a very cosmopolitan young woman who lived abroad for several years while working for a major corporation. A senior research scientist with her Ph.D. in organic chemistry, she is particularly looking forward to hosting international visitors, since she speaks fluent Italian and some French and even understands Spanish.

Worry not about safety in this neighborhood, for Bryan Place has an excellent security system, smoke alarms, and frequent police patrols. If you prefer a single bed, the hostess will rent her own downstairs bedroom. But please don't rearrange the two stakes and croquet balls by her bed, although she'll be interested in your intepretation of her artistic design. The room she usually uses for B&B guests is upstairs and has a queen-sized bed, cafe curtains, and an 1806 sepia etching. If you wish, a color television set can be brought in so you can watch your favorite shows in bed.

This room is just off an overhanging balcony that offers a breathtaking panorama of the living and dining rooms below. Extremely high vaulted ceilings take on added height with floor-to-ceiling ash paneling on the far wall, which has a built-in fireplace. Scattered about the polished parquet floors are Chinese medallion area rugs. The effect is smart and contemporary, although the furnishings include family heirlooms in addition to antiques acquired abroad. Architectural drawings done more than 150 years ago in Italy, a 1928 Tiffany-style vase, several handsome, heavy, signed brass pieces, and hand-carved chairs nearly a hundred years old that had been her grandmother's are a few items of interest.

A welcoming glass of sherry or wine will help you feel at home; a coffee maker is at your disposal. The pert young woman will fix a light breakfast before leaving early in the morning for work. Although preferring nonsmokers as B&B guests, Maria confides that you can smoke outside on the patio if you just can't resist. If you're traveling with Fifi or Fido, your pet will be welcome, for she has a small fenced-in yard, complete with one lone tree. Exall Park is across the street.

1 bedroom, 1 bath
Moderate
No smoking. No children.

BBTS NO. 7 (LAKEWOOD)

With a little prompting, the host of this elegant east Dallas home will tell you about the thirty-day sailing safari he made across the Atlantic in his thirty-five-foot sloop with his teenage son and another crewman. High adventure on the high seas! Tom has had many other exciting escapades in the *Lady Laura*, and maybe he'll tell you about them, too.

While the hostess enjoys sailing, English antiques are more her cup of tea. In fact, Rosemary owns an antique shop specializing in English antiques, and B&B guests are invited to go down and browse. Occasionally she displays some of the antiques from the shop at her spacious fifty-year-old Lakewood home, which she describes as Country English. Located across from Lakewood Country Club, the imposing two-story white colonial restored house has pillars in front and a big yard and swimming pool in back. The foyer has dramatic black and white diamond-shaped tile, reminiscent of the 1930s. A long, impressive carpeted staircase catches your eye immediately. The formal living room on the right is appealing, with a baby grand piano as the focal point; there is a fireplace in the well-appointed room, along with some period pieces.

The dining room has a fireplace, too, and it is usually lit on cold days so you can be warm as toast when you eat breakfast. Rosemary serves bacon and eggs, sausage, and toast on what else but English china. Tom sometimes prepares his special biscuits and gravy. Pour your coffee or tea from an individual silver service, which usually rests on the polished buffet.

Both guest rooms are upstairs. Rosemary rents only one room at a time unless travelers are together and don't mind sharing the bath in between. The front bedroom has a feminine antique white lace canopy over the fourposter double bed and lovely antique furniture. The adjoining bath reflects the hostess's fondness for rabbits. You'll see big rabbits, little rabbits, bunny rabbit wallpaper, and even a giant rabbit by the sink. The second room has brass and iron twin beds, which were Rosemary's when she was growing up. Her grandmother made the Victorian quilts. With a good view of the backyard and pool, this room is very pleasant, too.

To welcome each B&B guest, Rosemary and Tom write ahead, asking if there are any special attractions in Dallas their visitors would like to see; the hosts then offer to prepare an itinerary accordingly, which is a nice gesture. One of the oldest sections of Dallas, Lakewood has retained its charming identity. There are some gorgeous homes in the area, and you might want to drive around. It's only twenty minutes to downtown, and a public bus stops almost in front of the house. The hosts have two well-behaved Scotties, so they can't accept pets.

2 bedrooms, 1 bath
Moderate
No pets

BBTS NO. 8 (EAST DALLAS)

*W*hen these newlyweds discovered that both still had their baby plates, his with animals and hers with Baby Bunting, they knew that their marriage was meant to be. What makes it more remarkable that both should still have their baby plates—now displayed together in their east Dallas home—is that they are senior citizens. Marrying after a whirlwind courtship, Mary Lee and Glidden want to share their newfound happiness with B&B guests.

They have two rooms available. One has a walnut bedroom suite and throw rugs scattered around the hardwood floor. The double bed has a bookcase headboard with reading matter on a variety of subjects, including nature study. A huge Oriental hanging lamp over the bed makes a striking picture.

The second bedroom has a single chiropractic bed and a high-backed Spanish-style red velvet chair inherited from Mary Lee's mother, who incidentally was one of sixteen children! There is also a fifty-year-old drum table in the room and a framed but faded Oriental fan on the wall. The fan had been given to Mary Lee when she was a little girl by her mother, so it is something she cherishes. Actually, this bedroom doubles as a horticulture room and office for the hosts, who grow African violets and other plants in there.

The bathroom that these two rooms share is cherry red and pink with a black and gold Oriental mirror behind the commode. There are four other mirrors in the bathroom, giving it a dramatic effect.

Other Oriental accents in the one-story brick house include a silk embroidered picture of two peacocks, a cinnabar vase, an Oriental screen, and an Oriental figurine supposedly of a palace attendant. A palm reader once told Mary Lee that she had been an Oriental princess in another life, so maybe this is why she favors an Oriental motif.

The Texas-sized kitchen contains some interesting old pieces, too, such as a two-seater oak church pew from around 1914, acquired from a Lancaster church, and a 1915 rocker pictured in a Sears & Roebuck catalog of that year. You can sit in either while she fixes you a substantial breakfast of bacon and eggs, toast, and juice, and even hot or cold cereal if you wish.

The hosts, who have a true zest for life and many interests, have a piano and organ in the living room, and if you insist, Mary Lee will play a tune or two. You'll brighten her day, however, if you play for her! The hostess is also a skilled lapidarist who will be glad to show you the mineral specimens and rocks in her workshop.

Despite her busy days, Mary Lee will transport guests around Dallas on sightseeing tours, for a nominal fee. White Rock Lake, Tenison Golf Course, and Big Town and Town East malls are all near this B&B, which is about twenty minutes from downtown Dallas. The couple's home is not far from what used to be the Rinehart train stop, which was the first train stop out of Dallas coming east. Unfortunately, no historical marker designates what was once an important part of Dallas's history.

2 bedrooms, 1 bath
Moderate
No smoking. No children.
No pets

BBTS NO. 9 (MUNGER PLACE)

*B*uilt in the early 1900s as part of an exclusive development known as Munger Place, this stately dark red brick house has a Texas Historical Marker. Set far back from the wide boulevard several feet above street level, the imposing edifice has a side porte cochere and interesting symmetry. Its square-shaped pillars in front, long veranda, and exceptionally wide overhanging eaves make it an outstanding example of the Prairie School style of architecture made famous by Frank Lloyd Wright. The Prairie style is one of about sixteen distinct architectural styles identified in the Munger Place Historical District, which is one of the largest and most important examples of early twentieth-century homes existing in the Southwest and indeed the entire country. The district is listed on the National Register of Historic Places.

During World War II, many of the larger homes in Munger Place were converted into rooming houses and multifamily dwellings, which led to the decay of the neighborhood, accelerated by changes in the zoning laws. Thanks to monumental efforts by concerned residents and the Historic Preservation League in cooperation with city leaders, who passed new zoning guidelines, the irreplaceable homes have been returned to single-family status and their original grandeur.

Fortunately, this particular home has always been a single-family dwelling, retaining its identity and charm. Owned for about twenty-five years by a wealthy oilman who kept his oil leases in a safe that is still in the basement, the house then passed to his son and his daughter-in-law, a French woman who spent a great deal of money on its restoration and furnishings. In less than ten years, the couple sold the house to the parents of the B&B's host, who lived there for about thirty years. After residing in other states for many years, the present owners returned to Dallas and moved into the house eight years ago. Although Bill and Doris have been doing some redecorating, they have had to do little to the house itself. It looks as though it will last forever, and apparently it was built to do just that.

Who wouldn't be impressed by this jewel, with its high ceilings and hardwood floors (upstairs rooms are carpeted for warmth) and original brass light fixtures. Other features include three glass-enclosed sleeping porches, a finished attic with dormer windows that was formerly a playroom, and sun rooms adjoining each of the four bedrooms. Decorated with French and eighteenth-century pieces, the home will be fun to explore if you're an overnight B&B guest, especially since the hosts will make you feel so at home. This was the first home recruited by Bed & Breakfast Texas Style, by the way.

Stepping into the entrance foyer, you'll see that it's as big as most living rooms, with a hand-painted washbowl and pitcher in pastel pinks and blues sitting on a white marble-topped English table along with a decorative old candelabra. A treasured walnut Herschede grandfather's clock, two 200-year-old pulpit high chairs with gold velvet cushions, and a gold-leaf burl-front chest and mirror more than sixty years old are other attention-getters in the foyer. A silk and wool camel and royal blue–colored Oriental rug blends in well with the decor. This rug and another beautiful Oriental rug in the dining room are in as good condition today as they were when put down by the French woman years ago. She sold the rugs to Bill's parents along with the house. This second rug is pink and red with royal-blue accents. Ask Doris to show you the wiring for the buzzer, which in olden days was pressed to summon the downstairs or upstairs maid. It's under the rug.

The focal point of the formal living room to the right is a fireplace with a pink marble French mantel, another legacy of the French woman. Flanking the fireplace are two immense, very fine porcelain lamps, pink, green, and gold with ornate brass bases and unique scalloped shades crowned with

BBTS Number 9 (Munger Place)

lace. Doris and Bill were married in front of the fireplace more than thirty years ago.

The guest room on the second floor has an antique walnut French double bed with a cream-colored canopy trimmed with burgundy and matching dust ruffle and coverlet. A roll-up ladies' desk, a turn-of-the-century Swan Neck rocker, and an antique dresser are reminders of the past. Conveniences include a portable television, a telephone, and a sink right there in the room. Over the sink, enclosed in a walnut cabinet with a pink marble top, is an elongated old decorative mirror. A full bath is in between the adjoining second guest room and must be shared if both rooms are taken. The second room has a king-sized bed, a love seat, and plenty of closet space. The suite is ideal for couples traveling together or a family with children. (Teenage children are accepted.)

Although the days of upstairs and downstairs maids are long gone, you can be served breakfast in your room on a tray. Most prefer eating in the delightful morning room downstairs. The beveled glass panes on the French doors leading to the big yard and oversized pool in back catch the early morning sunlight. Breakfast sometimes includes a pumpkin custard topped with whipped cream, fresh fruit in sour cream, and blueberry muffins, homemade, of course.

Maybe you'll catch Bill playing a tune on the grand piano or organ in the nearby music room. His high-school drums are there, too. Don't overlook the 1889 music box, another family heirloom.

As a favor to B&B guests, the couple keeps literature on attractions in Dallas and restaurant guides. Their home is near a bus line and close to downtown Dallas, Fair Park, and White Rock Lake.

2 bedrooms, 1 bath
Moderate
No smoking. No pets.

BBTS NO. 10 (MUNGER PLACE)

*P*ractically all of the stately struc-
tures in the Swiss Avenue Historic District were once owned by the financial,
political, and cultural leaders of early Dallas. This spacious B&B is no exception. It was once the residence of Collett Munger, who developed much of
the area in the early 1900s with his brother, R. S. Munger. Swiss Avenue was
originally part of the 300-acre Munger Place development created in 1905.
The Mungers wanted Munger Place to be the "most attractive and desirable
residence in the entire South." And for more than forty years it was.

Although there were no zoning restrictions at the time, the Mungers de-
creed that all houses along Swiss Avenue must be two stories or more, cost at
least $10,000, and be located sixty to seventy feet from the front property
line. Thus they created the first restricted development in Texas. Naturally,
since this B&B was Collett Munger's own home, it met the criteria, and it too
has a historical marker.

Today Collett Munger's home is owned by a professional woman who has
been restoring it to its former grandeur. Another Frank Lloyd Wright Prairie
style design, shaded by towering trees, the buff brick home has an L-shaped
veranda, a side porte cochere, a second-floor balcony, and almost five thousand square feet of space, not to mention a huge, tree-shaded backyard. Pet-
rified wood is around the fish pond and along part of the driveway. Two giant
magnolia trees in front are gorgeous when in bloom.

The house has high ceilings throughout, as well as hardwood floors, beveled glass on the front door, and halls on both floors that are as big as most
living rooms. Old-fashioned radiators have been retained in the hall, although the house has central heat and air-conditioning.

The quaint downstairs guest room has an appliqued rose quilt made by Kathy's mother on the antique walnut double rope bed, which has acorn-shaped tops on the posters of the bed and the bottom feet as well. An antique armoire and chest of drawers, a night table, and a potty chair are in the room, which has rose drapes. White sheer lace curtains came from Prague. The bath is across the hall. If there is a third person in your party, a second room with a single bed is available on the second floor for a nominal fee.

By the way, the downstairs guest room was called the "lock room" by Collett Munger. During Prohibition, he kept his booze and valuables in this room under lock and key.

When you arrive, the gracious hostess will offer something to drink. Breakfast during the week will be something light like sweet rolls or English muffins, juice, coffee, perhaps bacon. On weekends, when she has more time, Kathy will fix scrambled eggs wrapped in a tortilla, or other hearty fare. Notice the beautiful handpainted china in the antique cabinet while you're eating in the cozy breakfast room. The twelve-piece place setting was painstakingly painted by Kathy's talented mom.

Swiss Avenue is close to the central business district, White Rock Lake, Fair Park, Baylor Medical Center, the renowned Dallas Theological Seminary, and major shopping areas and restaurants.

1 bedroom, 1 bath
Moderate
No children. No pets.

BBTS Number 10 (Munger Place)

BBTS NO. 11 (NORTH DALLAS)

*I*n the old days, peddlers often made a cookie cutter for the children instead of paying for lodging at an inn. A number of these antique cookie cutters are among the many collectibles in this spellbinding north Dallas B&B, which has wall-to-wall Victorian and early Americana antiques as well. Take a trip down memory lane as Gwen tells about each treasure and how it came to be in her possession. Some of her stories are priceless. For instance, she reveals how her husband saw a truck parked in front of a saloon when they were living in Ohio years ago. Going in, Jack found the driver and asked if the table in the back of the truck was for sale. The driver asked Jack how much he had in his pocket. Jack said, "$1.75," and the obliging man said it was his. Some of their other cherished antiques have been obtained for almost nothing, too, like a rare pine chest that Gwen got at an auction for only $5. At the time, its beauty was hidden beneath eight coats of paint, but Gwen realized what was there. Its gorgeous marble top was added by her grandfather, a stonemason.

A slat church pew with kneeling bench intact that came from an old Catholic church in Arkansas, a snizzle (an antique tool) dating from the 1840s, and an old icebox with shelves are a few of her other favorites. It took Gwen two and a half years to scrape the layers of paint off the latter with a toothbrush, by the way. Also on display is a beaded picture frame that her grandfather accepted from an Indian on the Kansas prairie in return for food in the early 1800s. Just inside the front door to the right is a tiny Victorian music room with an old pump organ, a miniature love seat, and 1890 hymnbooks.

The guest room has its share of treasures, including a birds-eye maple trundle bed (a single) and a spinet desk that folds up, along with antique dolls that belonged to the couple's daughter. In the bath, which must be shared with the family, is the three-sided shaving mirror that was Kathy's grandfather's. In the hall by the bedroom are a number of other interesting items, including her dad's spats and his father's derby.

You'll eat breakfast, which often includes a delicious egg and cheese casserole and special muffins, at the kitchen counter, sitting not on an ordinary stool but on an old-fashioned milk can. As Gwen prepares breakfast, examine her collectibles in the kitchen, which include candy molds, measuring cups, bread pans, old cooking utensils, and more.

The yard is as special as the house. The avid collector has multicolored glass insulators that were used on telephone poles in years gone by. Kathy has them strung across the top of a rustic wood dividing wall that has a grape-vine-covered top. (Maybe you'll sample wine made from the green grapes.) Giant six-foot-tall elephant ears, a cactus that blooms at night, a whiskey barrel with water plants and fish, hanging baskets dangling from the trees, year-round flowers, and blooming plants make this a veritable Garden of Eden. Sitting on the wooden patio deck as the sun goes down will make your spirits soar. Mittens, the family's cat, thinks this is quite a place, too.

Promenade Center in Richardson is close by, but other malls like Preston-wood, Valley View, and Olla Podrida are easy to get to from this fascinating B&B as well.

1 bedroom, 1 bath
Moderate
No smoking. No pets.

BBTS NO. 12 (NORTH DALLAS)

*I*f you like to shop, this north Dallas contemporary home would be a great place to stay, for it is only about five minutes away from three of the city's finest malls—Valley View, Preston-wood, and the Galleria. The nearby Dallas Toll Road provides quick and easy access to downtown Dallas or even Market Hall.

Quilting has been a family passion for several generations, and some handsome quilts are displayed as wall hangings and cleverly used as table-cloths, along with crocheted doilies and such for a very pleasing effect. There is even a blue and yellow quilt, recently made by the hostess, on the queen-sized bed in the guest room. The bed has an antique reproduction frame. Tastefully furnished with a country look, the guest room and private bath are separated from the master suite by the living room, den, and kitchen, so you'll have lots of privacy.

There is a mini-bar with soft drinks, an icemaker, and a hot-water gadget in the den, so you can make yourself coffee, hot chocolate, or tea, or get water or a soft drink whenever you wish. Jack and Lois, who enjoy meeting new people, want you "to feel our home is your home away from home."

Sit by the fire in the winter or on the patio in back on warmer days. The secluded backyard is charming, with its vine-covered lattice cedar frame, flowers and greenery, hanging baskets, a bench, and an umbrella-covered table where you can eat breakfast in the morning or just enjoy a beautiful sunset at night. On more leisurely weekends, you're apt to get a country breakfast, complete with eggs, sausage, and seasonal fruit, but a continental breakfast will be served during the week.

Park off the street under the porte cochere in front. If you need transportation, the hostess will help out for a nominal fee. You'll be comfortable and safe here, for there is an excellent security system in the well-appointed house. Suzette, a friendly white poodle, bids you welcome, too.

1 bedroom, 1 bath
Moderate
No smoking. No children.
No pets

BBTS NO. 13 (NORTH DALLAS)

*B*reakfast is stylish at this north Dallas B&B, on white china dishes, black lace placemats, and the finest crystal. It's fun choosing what you want from an elaborate menu the night before, with offerings ranging from Sara Lee pecan coffee cake to scrambled or fried eggs, English muffins, and yogurt. The menu is written on a Dennis the Menace card that says, "I'm just sticking around to see what happens next."

You will, too, for the energetic hostess goes out of her way to make sure that each and every B&B guest has a pleasant stay. If you like, she'll even come up with a late-night snack, usually cheese and crackers. A nice home on the corner with a towering ash tree in the yard, this B&B has three guest rooms, all with access to an individual bath.

One cheerful room is a sunny yellow with a double bed, an easy chair, and a radio. It overlooks a plant-filled sun room, making it kind of special. A second room has ducks on display, so a sportsman would enjoy it. This room has a single bed, an old-fashioned highboy for clothes, and fabric on the wall, while the third room has French Provincial furniture, blue, silver, white, and gold wallpaper, and family portraits for you to see. There are telephone jacks in all three, so a telephone can easily be moved into your room for privacy.

Mary, the hostess, had traveled throughout the world with her husband, a colonel in the Marine Corps who served as director of civil defense for Dallas after his retirement, and some furnishings were acquired abroad. For instance, there is a finger tray and rosewood screen from India, a teakwood dining room table and buffet from Denmark, a 1962 German pound, and a coffee pot exactly like the one used on stage and in the movie of *Lawrence of Arabia*. She honors her husband's memory with his medals showcased under a glass-topped table in the living room. Incidentally, he once ate dinner with King Hussein while serving on the admiral's staff of the commander-in-chief of the Mediterranean. Mary has other stories she can tell about their interesting life and travels.

A woman of many interests, Mary likes painting, sewing, and ceramics. Although you probably won't find her waltzing around the house, dancing is another passion. So is her black poodle, Beau Jangles, who more readily answers to his nickname, B. J. No doubt he'll try to make friends with you.

Only minutes from Dallas Parkway and not far from the Toll Road and LBJ Expressway, this B&B is in an ideal location no matter where you want to go in Dallas. Mary will even help you make dinner reservations if you wish.

3 bedrooms, 3 baths
Moderate
No smoking. No children.
No pets

BBTS NO. 14 (NORTH DALLAS)

A clubhouse with a sauna, tennis courts, and not one but five swimming pools are a few of the amenities that will make your stay memorable at this beautifully landscaped Country French townhome in north Dallas. Realizing that most travelers don't cart along paraphernalia like bikes and tennis rackets, the gracious hosts offer to lend you their own. Take advantage of the nature trails in back or the jogging, exercise, and bicycling course at nearby Bachman Lake.

Elegantly furnished with a contemporary look, the townhome has a wrought-iron gate in back and a small courtyard. In the alcove is a Chinese figurine, which represents, appropriately enough, the goddess of mercy and hospitality. The figurine is visible from the cozy breakfast nook. A grand piano dominates the formal living and dining room area, which contains travel mementos such as a rice paper temple rubbing and hand-carved bone elephants from Thailand.

The hosts are well-educated, widely traveled bachelors in their mid-thirties who hope to own a country inn one day. In the meantime, visitors from this country and abroad are invited to stay in their spacious guest suite on the second floor of their luxurious townhome. They especially hope to welcome more international guests like the textile manufacturer from Germany and the research librarian from Ireland who stayed there while attending conventions in Dallas.

Exceptionally large, with a queen-sized bed, a huge walk-in closet with built-in shelves, and a dressing area with double sinks, the guest room is at the opposite end of the long hall from the master suite, so your privacy is assured. Just ask, and a television can be set up in your room, but there is a comfortable chair in case you'd like to read, as well as a small refrigerator for cool drinks and snacks. The guest room has a balcony that overlooks a grassy meadow and bird-filled trees. City life will seem far away, but it isn't.

The central business district, the rapidly growing Las Colinas Urban Center, and the LBJ and Addison office complexes are within easy driving distance, while Love Field is no more than a ten-minute, $5 cab ride. It takes about fifteen minutes longer to get to DFW. There is good bus service to downtown Dallas, and the hosts hope you'll take time to explore the fabulous new Dallas Museum of Art. Oak Lawn, an interesting, more Bohemian potpourri of specialty shops, clubs, and restaurants, as well as shopping meccas such as the Galleria, Sakowitz Village, and Valley View, are all close enough to make this B&B a good base for your Dallas visit.

Your visit will include a welcoming glass of sherry and a light breakfast during the week, with omelets, bacon, ham, or sausage, pastries, and cereal as typical weekend offerings. Check what you want on a printed menu the night before, and your wish is your hosts' command.

1 bedroom, 1 bath
Moderate
No smoking. No children.
No pets

BBTS NO. 15 (NORTH DALLAS)

*A*fter staying in bed and breakfast inns while touring England and Scotland several years ago, George and Betty came home sold on the concept. Now they extend their own hospitality to visitors from this country and abroad in their north Dallas home. The ecstatic golfing addicts say this is like "being paid to have a party."

Breakfasting with guests is part of the fun, claim the couple. One guest felt so at home that he even fixed breakfast for them during his week-long stay. Even if you don't ordinarily eat heavily in the morning, resisting such tempting possibilities as Betty's jalapeño muffins and jelly and George's special scrambled eggs will be difficult. Perhaps that's because the hosts are so congenial and the atmosphere so inviting. Eating on the plant-filled atrium porch that overlooks the yard is a favorite with B&B guests.

The contemporary eclectic home includes family treasures such as a rocking-horse chair by the hearth in the living room. A true primitive, it has raised five generations. Over the fireplace is a child's orange linen-like dress, made by slaves for Betty's great-grandmother on their farm in Missouri around a hundred and twenty years ago. A potpourri of precious items like family pictures taken at the 1904 World's Fair in St. Louis and old locks are in a glass-covered table. Displayed in the dining room are framed calling and Christmas cards from olden years, while an antique hand-carved pier mirror stands out in the hall.

Multicolored antique fans, all open and placed at angles to each other, cover almost all the walls in the first of three guest rooms. The fan room has twin beds. If you're a Republican, you'll love the second B&B room, which has a patriotic red, white, and blue decor, an elephant madras wall hanging from Pakistan, and an antique table and quill. The couple collects elephant images, and some are in this room. A third room is larger than these two. Adjoining the atrium porch, it has an antique four-poster double bed and chest. All three rooms have private baths and television sets. A portacrib is available.

Like other north Dallas B&Bs, this home is near prestigious shopping malls such as Prestonwood and the Galleria and easily accessible to downtown Dallas and Market Hall. The University of Texas at Dallas, where the hostess works, is nearby. Southfork isn't far, either.

3 bedrooms, 3 baths
Moderate
No restrictions

BBTS NO. 16 (NORTHEAST DALLAS)

*T*his effervescent hostess has opened not only her home but also her heart to her B&B guests. Genuinely concerned that each have an enjoyable stay, Polly and her gracious husband, Bill, go out of their way to make guests feel like family. From the minute Polly opens the door of their contemporary Spanish-style northeast Dallas home to the last goodbye, you'll bask in the warmth of the outgoing couple's hospitality. It is this feeling of conviviality that makes staying here so memorable.

Guests have the run of the kitchen and the house itself. Invite friends over, if you wish, or even have a dinner party. Warm your feet before the fire on a cold winter night, maybe watch television. The coffee pot is always on, so help yourself, says Polly, who fixes fancy coffee drinks and special omelets at breakfast. For a nominal fee, the accommodating hostess will perform extra services, such as taking guests on city tours and shopping expeditions and providing transportation to and from the airport and around town. Taking her guests under her wing, this lively lady even helped one young woman househunt. And Bill, a former newspaperman who now has his own employment agency, found a job for one B&B guest. Guests even join them for church.

"Hearth, home, and heart. That's what B&B is all about," says Polly. The fire that destroyed their last home and prized possessions did not dampen their zest for life. All of the furnishings in their spacious home now are new. Characterized by informal elegance, the house has three bedrooms for B&B guests, and all three have television sets. To the left of the living room is a bedroom suite, which has a double bed plus a sofa that can sleep two more, if children are along. The room is not fancy, but it is comfortable and has a private bath. The laundry room is next to it, and you're welcome to do your wash if you're staying any length of time.

The other two guest rooms are to the right of the living room and share an adjoining bath. One is a sunny room with a Spanish decor in orange, green, and gold. The double bed is new, but the feather pillows are twenty-five years old. Her grandmother's down pillows are in all three guest rooms, by the way. The third bedroom has a double bed, too, and a small French window.

Polly and Bill have an extensive library, if you'd like to read, and a video recorder to tape any programs you wish while you're out. Their home is easily accessible from major thoroughfares like LBJ, Northwest Highway, and North Central Expressway, and only a block away from a bus stop. Valley View, NorthPark, and Olla Podrida are a few of the great malls within easy driving distance.

3 bedrooms, 2 baths
Moderate
No smoking

BBTS NO. 17 (NORTHEAST DALLAS)

*T*his imposing trilevel stone, brick, and cedar contemporary home, which is on a corner in northeast Dallas, has a host of amenities, including a huge swimming pool and a game room with a pool table and picnic table. You'll enjoy yourself here! After raising five children who were all teenagers at the same time, the hosts have opened their splendid home to B&B guests, when they're not off on a jaunt themselves, that is.

On the front porch is an old-fashioned red school desk, while the door knocker says, "Peace to all who enter here." This will immediately make you feel at home. Sentimentalists will enjoy this B&B, for two of the three guest rooms, which are all up some stairs to the left, are filled with family treasures. Among the cherished heirlooms in the first room is a double-sized spool bed that had belonged to Gail's grandmother and great-grandmother before that. A rose and dusty blue ruffled comforter with a blue dust ruffle matches the pillow on a nearby chair and the skirt on the round lamp table, so the decor has a designer look. For cool nights, there is a quilt made by her 101-year-old grandmother, who lives in Arkansas. The frilly white Priscilla curtains are precious, too, for they came from the back porch of her two old-maid aunts. The room, which overlooks the pool, has a television, a telephone, and an adjoining full bath.

A long hall lined with book-filled shelves leads to the other two guest rooms. One has an antique queen-sized bed, a dresser, and a crib and is more masculine-looking than the first. The third room has two single beds and a long built-in desk, making it ideal for study or work. There are televisions and telephones in both these rooms, which share a bath. A small refrigerator is available for any of the three guest rooms, if you wish.

If you enjoy chess, a game table is set up in a small nook at the top of the stairs. Peer over the balcony to the den below, an impressive view. Pass through a small living room with an organ to reach the den, where the host often plunks away on a banjo. A retired American Airlines captain, he now owns a Lower Greenville Avenue nightspot called the Saloon, one of only three clubs in the country that feature bluegrass music. There is a fireplace in the den, which you're welcome to enjoy on cold nights.

On weekends, the hosts sometimes fix a Tex-Mex omelet, but they usually serve fresh fruit and juice along with croissants or delicious ham and cheese pastries from a nearby French pastry shop.

Within walking distance of a library, this B&B home is also close to many of Dallas's top restaurants and nightspots, several shopping malls like North-Park and Valley View, and area attractions such as White Water. About a mile from LBJ and Central Expressways, it is also convenient to a bus line.

Even though claiming that their home is childproof after raising five of their own, they prefer not to take children, but will accept babies. Small pets are also welcome. (Please, no Great Danes!)

3 bedrooms, 2 baths
Moderate
No children

BBTS NO. 18 (OAK CLIFF)

A beautiful weeping willow and a variety of plants and flowers frame this comfortable, one-story brick home in Oak Cliff, which some say is the most scenic part of Dallas, with its rolling hills and wooded terrain. Located south of the Trinity River, Oak Cliff has a fine freeway network that will have you in downtown Dallas, at the apparel mart, or anywhere else in nothing flat. Though the Galleria, Prestonwood, and other major malls north of the river might seem alluring, Oak Cliff has a fine mall of its own—Redbird—as well as other attractions such as the Dallas Zoo, Lake Cliff Park, and revitalized historic neighborhoods like Winnetka Heights. Because of its proximity to downtown, Oak Cliff has been experiencing a resurgence that boosters hope will help restore the status that the close-knit community held in olden days.

There are several B&Bs in the southwest quadrant of Dallas County, but this one is closest to town. The outgoing hosts have lived in Oak Cliff ever since he became pastor of a church here about five years ago. Visiting with guests before the fireplace or in the den makes participating in the B&B program rewarding. (They especially enjoyed a doctor who told about jumping off a Communist ship to freedom.)

A quilt made by Iola's mother and one of her own crewel pillows are on the double bed in one of the guest rooms, along with an easy chair, a radio, a telephone, and lots of closet space and drawers for your convenience. The private bath must be shared if a second room down the hall has B&B guests.

Behind the bed is a window with a great view of their fantastic backyard. Once flat, it has now been transformed by the couple into a sloping garden with seven terraces. Railroad ties add to the rustic charm. "We refer to our backyard as 'Mohammed's Mountain,'" quip the hosts. In one corner is an herb garden.

Their second bedroom is larger and has a queen-sized bed. Be forewarned: A stuffed badger, teeth and fangs bared, is on the bed as a conversation piece. This delightful critter is a memento from her daddy's tannery. A small trampoline and a spot reducer are also in the room, and you're welcome to use them.

That will be one way to work up a good appetite for the hearty breakfast of scrambled eggs, huevos rancheros, or an herb omelet (the herbs are from their garden, naturally), plus homemade bread and jelly. The bread and jelly are made by a member of their church.

If you have time, the jovial hosts will tell you about some of their interesting possessions, such as three pieces of carnival glass from the 1913 Gillespie County Fair, still held each year in her hometown, Fredericksburg. Also interesting are his grandfather's Dresden shaving mug, an 1891 buffet, a grandfather clock that Walter made himself, and an oil painting of the smokehouse behind her family's homestead. On the mantel is her father's big 1913 German Bible, always open to passages such as Christmas. (Both Walter and Iola are fluent in German.) In the corner of the dining room is an étagère that displays gifts or collectibles from twenty-five countries, such as a cloisonné vase from Japan. Iola calls the étagère "my corner of the world."

Don't think that just because Walter is a minister you'll have to mind your Ps and Qs more than usual. These are fun people! "Unique" (part poodle, part Scottish terrier) will help you feel at home in this very pleasant B&B.

2 bedrooms, 1 bath
Moderate
No smoking. No children.
No pets

BBTS NO. 19 (OLD EAST DALLAS)

*O*range marigolds add a dash of color to the greenery on one side of this U-shaped Old East Dallas home—a new home with an old look. The host, who designed and built it himself about six years ago, explains that it is a reproduction of the architectural style typical of his historic Junius Heights neighborhood. Though the grey brick and frame exterior blends in with others on his block (some have been restored, others haven't), it stands out. A circular driveway makes it look more chic, even though it's built fairly close to the street to make maximum use of the small lot. Tom built his beloved house after the city changed the zoning laws to attract responsible single-family homeowners back to the inner-city neighborhood, which had deteriorated into multifamily units. Many of the homes were built about sixty years ago.

You'll be captivated by his window treatment. Instead of curtains, this creative B&B host has hung three striking stained-glass panes in two long, narrow panels in front. There are no curtains to wash, and sunlight pours through the stained glass, bathing the house with light. A small square-shaped stained-glass pane hangs in the tiny window above the porch, as well.

The house has been featured on "CBS Morning News," "Good Morning America," and other television shows, in conjunction with Tom's participation in Bed & Breakfast Texas Style. Although it is of the old style of architecture, it has a contemporary look inside. Floors are of Mexican tile, and the interior "walls" around a rustic wooden decked patio are all glass. It's nice to view this plant-filled courtyard as you move from room to room.

Just made for easy living and entertaining, the house has an eclectic decor, with an eighteenth-century rocker, an old English hat stand, and other antiques attractively interspersed with more modern pieces and mementos from Tom's extensive travels abroad. A personnel consultant specializing in the data processing area, he collects works of young Texas artists, which are displayed throughout the interesting house.

A fully equipped electric kitchen with a Jenn-Aire range is the focal point for Tom, a gourmet cook who fixes continental breakfasts for B&B guests during the week but something more elaborate on weekends when he doesn't have to work. He quickly points out that his kitchen, which has an island counter, may be small, but it's compact and designed for maximum efficiency.

The guest room is nothing fancy, but it's comfortable, clean, and private. Referred to as the "blue room," since it has blue wallpaper, it has a double brass bed and a private bath. There is no television in the room, but Tom doesn't want you in there watching TV. He hopes you'll spend your spare time getting acquainted. After all, he became a B&B host just to chat with the intriguing people who stay in homes like his. You're welcome to use the swimming pool in back or relax awhile beneath the big umbrella that shades the canary yellow and navy blue striped lawn furniture on the courtyard patio, which is surrounded by plants and hanging baskets. A wind chime will tinkle in the breeze. On wintry nights, warm yourself by the built-in fireplace in the living room. A sweet-natured Sheltie named Tillie will help you feel at home.

A bus line is only a half block away, while downtown Dallas, the new Museum of Art, the arts district—Fair Park—and White Rock Lake are a few of the city's attractions close to this appealing B&B.

1 bedroom, 1 bath
Budget
No children. No pets.

Denton

BBTS NO. 20

*T*his remarkable home filled with antiques will keep you busy every minute trying to encompass all the beautiful hand-carved furniture and interesting artifacts. You won't know where to look first. Hilda and L. N. have enlarged their home twice just to accommodate their collections. Though every nook and cranny is crammed with something precious, the North Texas home is extremely livable. The hosts enjoy their possessions and hope you will, too.

Probably the most impressive pieces are five absolutely gorgeous antique sideboards, which Hilda plans to pass along to their five grandchildren. One ten-foot-high beauty was smuggled from the Russian zone of Berlin by its former owner, a friend of their daughter, who was living overseas at the time. Ask Hilda to tell you the story.

With pride, Hilda points out a barley twist teakwood table in the living room, explaining that the legs have been twisted by hand, not machine. Some of their furniture has marble tops that were custom made by L. N., a skilled craftsman. An old tea cart and coal box purchased in England are other items of interest.

Look carefully, or you'll miss something tucked away under a table or even up on the rafters. See the old stagecoach light and buffalo gun suspended from the vaulted ceiling. You name it, and this couple probably has a collection of it in spades, including sea shells from Hawaii, the Philippines, and other exotic places; old keys and locks from European castles they've visited; prints, brass knobs, and rubbings from England; even cowboy and Indian figurines. There are ducks, owls, and other animal collections, but the most cherished are probably the hundred-year-old very heavy hand-carved wooden elephants from Africa on the mantel above the brick fireplace in the living room. These came from an estate sale in London but were originally given to the Englishman by an African tribesman long ago.

In one corner of the living room, incidentally, are an organ, a set of drums, a tambourine, and a guitar kept on hand for their grandchildren; if you feel like playing any of the instruments, go to it!

You'll enjoy the ritzy guest quarters, too, which include a private entrance and a small bath. A sitting room and bedroom, separated by a semiwall, are elegantly furnished in American antiques and reproductions. Next to the king-sized bed is one of the more novel pieces, a cherrywood wagon-train rocker with a needlepoint cushion. (In olden days, pioneers folded the rocker up so it would take up less space on the wagon.) The sitting room includes a sleigh couch, an easy-chair rocker, another barley twist table, and a beautiful leaded antique vase. And a television!

If a family has a child, they might prefer a back bedroom. Besides the king-sized bed, a couch in an adjoining sitting area can be made into a bed. If you need a crib, just ask. This is one of the few B&Bs that accepts smokers, children, and pets. (Pets stay in a dog run out back.)

A full breakfast will be served. The kitchen should prove interesting, too, for it has two double sinks and tile cabinets. When the house was enlarged once, a new kitchen was installed and the old one retained. Because they frequently entertain, the extra sinks and countertops come in handy, says Hilda.

Located just off the major freeway that bisects Denton, this special B&B is within six blocks of both North Texas State University and Texas Woman's University. Both schools have interesting museums.

1 bedroom, 1 bath
Moderate
No restrictions

DeSoto

*I*f you enjoyed listening to old radio shows like "I Love a Mystery," "Suspense," and "Amos and Andy," you'll have a ball at this B&B in DeSoto, a suburb in southwest Dallas County. The host has a huge collection of not only old radio shows such as these but also a variety of films from yesteryear, and he'll gladly share them with you. If you have time, he'll treat you to an evening film fest, showing a cartoon, a preview of coming attractions, a newsreel, and a main feature—the same lineup you would have seen at the movies forty years ago for a quarter. Just tell Tommy what you want to see, and you've got it, with maybe some popcorn to boot.

The radio shows, film tapes, and a massive record collection that includes big band sounds and hits by the Sons of the Pioneers are stored in one room. Flip through bound volumes of old Walt Disney comics in there, too. A talented musician himself (though a banker by profession), Tommy also writes hymns, and some have been recorded. A framed copy of one hymn is on display. He corresponds with radio and film collectors all over the world. Maybe some of them will wind up at his home as a B&B guest one day.

Tommy and Joyce's recently redecorated guest room has a double bed, an easy chair, and an adjoining bath with a double sink. This is probably one of the more modest homes registered with Bed & Breakfast Texas Style, but undoubtedly one of the more fascinating. A grandfather clock, some tables, and a curio cabinet, all made by the host, are among items of interest.

Both Tommy and Joyce have traveled extensively and have home movies of trips to Hawaii, Europe, and New England. But don't worry. You won't have to watch these—unless, of course, you ask. Hooked on staying at B&Bs themselves, the couple bought a multicolored hand-blown lamp in New England with what they saved by not staying in motels but in bed and breakfast homes.

Because both work, you'll get a continental breakfast during the week, but on Saturday or Sunday Tommy will cook up a storm. On nice days, breakfast is served on the patio. The couple welcomes older children, and smokers only if they confine smoking to their guest room. Though they are warm and friendly, their dog is not, so please don't try to pet ol' Skipper!

DeSoto, by the way, is situated near both Interstate Highways 35 and 20 and is about fifteen minutes from downtown Dallas.

1 bedroom, 1 bath
Moderate
No pets

Duncanville

*P*ing-pong, anyone? The host of this lovely Duncanville B&B challenges guests to a game, but be forewarned that he's a champion player who even makes his own paddles. Taking him on isn't obligatory, of course, but it might be fun, especially if you catch him on an off day and win. In any case, you should work up a good appetite for the delicious homemade dessert his wife will serve that night.

Perhaps you'll prefer to pass up ping-pong in favor of the inviting-looking hammock strung between two tall pine trees in back. Or relax in the redwood furniture on the wooden deck and watch the squirrels and raccoons play among the brush or by the creek. Two old-fashioned milk cans are attention-getters in the beautiful yard. You can enjoy all this natural beauty from the breakfast nook in the morning, too, because it has big bay windows. Breakfast is usually light during the week, but something more substantial, like a mushroom or cheese omelet, will be whipped up on weekends.

The hosts are transplanted midwesterners who entertain and travel often and have a second home in Colorado. Their house is on a hilly street in a quiet residential neighborhood. There are two adjoining guest rooms, so if you're traveling with friends or family, this B&B might suit you to a T. The larger room has a king-sized bed and a lot of atmosphere. Strung across the ceiling from one end of the room to the other is a fishnet filled with tiny stuffed animals that belonged to the couple's three daughters. Teddy bears and other animals are tucked into corners, too. There is a stereo. The second room has twin beds and is available for a little less. The bathroom is shared if both rooms are taken. The family cat and dog might wander in.

Staying at this B&B is something to consider if you have business anywhere in southwest Dallas County, or even Fort Worth or Dallas, since Duncanville is about a twenty-minute drive from each. A growing Dallas suburb of about thirty thousand, Duncanville offers easy access to major attractions such as Six Flags, Texas Stadium, and the Texas Rangers. DFW Airport is about twenty-five minutes away. The Greenhill Environmental Center in Duncanville might also be of interest. Open from sunrise to sunset seven days a week, the nature preserve has a wildflower festival each May. Explore the nature trails yourself or call ahead for a guided tour.

2 bedrooms, 1 bath
Moderate
No smoking. No pets.

Flower
Mound

*C*asa Cabrito ("house of the little goat"), one of the more novel B&Bs, is situated on a country road in the tiny hamlet of Flower Mound in southern Denton County. (More about Flower Mound later.) Originally a feed shed and tack room, the small but compact one-room cottage includes a double bed, a sitting area, a neat kitchenette, a dining area, and of course a bathroom with shower, which is in back by the bed. Everything you could possibly want or need has been provided by the thoughtful hosts, who live just across the way in a handsome sixty-year-old frame house, probably the oldest in the area. A white rail fence weaves around the house and Casa Cabrito, separating both from pastureland that the young couple also own. "Rancho Bravado," the name of their five-acre spread, is inscribed on the arch over the white rail gate in front of the main house. Their three horses, a golden retriever, a springer spaniel, and other assorted pets wander around, obviously relishing life in this postcard-pretty setting. On weekends, when the couple isn't working, you can ride the horses, if you like. All kinds of pets, even horses, are welcome here.

201

If you're looking for an offbeat, comfortable country retreat, this is it. Actually, it's not as isolated as it sounds; Casa Cabrito is only about fifteen minutes from DFW Airport, which is why so many airline pilots and businesspeople have been discovering this charming B&B. Occasionally the host can provide transportation to and from the airport in his vintage automobile.

Believe it or not, Casa Cabrito has both a front door and a glass-paned back door—just opposite each other—in addition to two windows and a skylight; so the room seems airy and light. If you're tall, watch your head when you enter; even though the roof was raised four inches when the cottage was converted from a tack room, the ceiling is still relatively low. This makes a delightful getaway for two, but bring the children if you like, for two comfortable chairs plus a blue sleeper sofa can be converted into beds. There are lots of animal figurines and pictures around, including a ceramic pig over the cabinet. Air-conditioned and heated, the cottage even contains a color television and a super stereo.

The compact kitchenette has a small refrigerator, a sink, a three-burner stove, a good-sized oven, and even a small storage area. You'll find ample makings for a hearty breakfast even for just a one-night visit, but stay two nights or more and you'll find a dozen eggs, homemade Danish, freshly squeezed orange juice, fresh mixed fruits, pancake mix, a variety of cereals, and a good selection of coffee, jasmine and mint tea, and marmalade and preserves. All B&B guests also get wine or champagne as an added treat, plus cheese and crackers and other snack food, not to mention candy, nuts, and fresh flowers. Talk about pampered—at no extra cost, either!

Don't think that this is only a fair-weather retreat, for the sound of raindrops falling on the tin roof makes Casa Cabrito seem even more romantic. It even has a resident ghost, who seemed quite harmless to David when he saw the old man sitting in a chair next to the glass-topped table where you'll eat. Melita, who formerly was publisher and editor of a local paper, says that her husband, a Naval Academy graduate who is a sales executive, isn't the kind to conjure up something like this, but she's never seen the ghost. Who knows, maybe you will.

Located about thirty-five minutes from Denton and just a trifle longer to downtown Dallas or Fort Worth, Flower Mound is an interesting place. There actually is a mound, just off the farm-to-market road about two miles from Casa Cabrito. A Texas Historical Marker is at the site, which rises about fifty feet above the surrounding prairie. It's owned by the Mound Corporation, composed of longtime Flower Mound residents who have been instrumental in preserving the mound. The geological feature itself was named for the profusion of wildflowers that usually bloom on it. Supposedly this is where the

Wichita Indians gathered for council meetings in the early 1800s. According to the legend, nothing must ever be constructed on the sacred site, and nothing ever has, although there have been several attempts. In the 1870s, material was stacked on the mound until needed for construction of a new building for the historic Flower Mound Presbyterian Church, organized a few years before by early-day settlers. A tornado swept across the mound, flinging the material around like straw. Reputedly the same thing later happened to lumber and framing for a house about to be built on the mound. And strangely enough, though wildflowers crop up in great numbers most years, no tree planted there has ever survived. The legend of Flower Mound lives on.

Contact Bed & Breakfast Hosts
of San Antonio
166 Rockhill
San Antonio 78209
(512) 824-8036
1 bedroom, 1 bath
Exclusive
No restrictions

Fort Worth

*W*ith its marvelous museums, Botanical Gardens, and impressive convention center, which spans fourteen downtown blocks, Fort Worth has long had a fan club of its own. Billy Bob's and the restored stockyards have been making it even more of a mecca for tourists, and this one-story brick B&B home is only about four miles from both. If you need a break from work or play, cool off in the hosts' unusual designer pool, which even has a diving board. The yard is fenced in, so you can swim in private.

There are two guest rooms, but a third can be used if it is needed, especially for children. Actually the office of the hostess—a brick mason—the latter has a studio bed. The first guest room has a queen-sized bed. Both the headboard and walls are decorated with the same padded fabric—black with soft green and gold flowers, looking somewhat Oriental and very appealing. The second room is a little larger, with red velvet draperies and a matching spread on the double bed. If you have business to catch up on at night, this room would be great, for it has a desk-dresser as well as a sewing machine del Sol as a bed and breakfast home and serve a continental breakfast. However, the ranch house is also available for business conferences, Christmas cabinet that can double as a desk. Because the bath in the hall must be shared, the hosts rent only to one family or those traveling in the same party. Continental or full breakfast—the choice is yours.

Located in a new addition on the northeast side of Fort Worth, near both Interstate Highway 20 and IH 35 West, this comfortable home is only about six miles from downtown. Despite her busy schedule working with her husband, the hostess volunteers to arrange transportation and tours for B&B guests. (A nominal fee will be added for this service.) She's proud of her city, which is striving for a more sophisticated image, though Fort Worth can hold its own with any city in the country, with the Amon G. Carter Museum of Western Art (Remington and Russell are featured), the Kimbell Art Museum, the Fort Worth Museum of Science and History, and other outstanding museums, all within a small area.

The Southwestern Exposition Fat Stock Show and Rodeo, held annually in late January or early February, reflects the western heritage of the city, which became a major shipping and supply depot for cattlemen after the Civil War. Octoberfest in October and the Colonial Golf Classic in May are other events that might be of interest if you're staying at this B&B. Casa Mañana Theater, a theater in the round under an intriguing geodesic dome, offers drama, musical comedies, and other entertainment through the year.

2 bedrooms, 1 bath
Moderate
No pets

Garland

BBTS NO. 24

*I*t was the depression, and Mexican laborers asked only for food and a place to sleep in return for building a sprawling, Spanish-style hacienda for T. C. Brown, an honorary Texas Ranger. Secluded amid rare, 500-year-old oak trees on the renowned Spring Creek Nature Preserve in, of all places, Garland, a suburb only thirty minutes from downtown Dallas, Casa del Sol today retains its charm of old.

Recognized by a historic medallion and patterned after a large Mexican estate, Casa del Sol ("House of the Sun") has four bedrooms, two connecting party rooms that can comfortably accommodate about fifty, several cozy dens, a kitchen (feel free to bring food for dinner), even an altar room hidden beneath the stairs. With a fish pond in front and a creek in back, three massive Austin limestone fireplaces, visual treats like the graceful archways that separate some of the rooms, a mosaic blue and white tiled porch, and Mexican Art Deco throughout, this is a special retreat indeed.

T. C. Brown enjoyed his hacienda for thirty-five years, finally selling it in 1950 to the present owners. Their daughter, Ann, and her husband run Casa parties, family reunions, and special occasions such as weddings. (Like Ann, you can marry before the hundred-year-old hand-carved altar inside or take your vows at the chapel—a huge rock altar—in the woods, only a stone's throw from the house.)

The front entrance leads directly to a spacious suite, which has a crystal chandelier over the canopy-covered double bed. A couch opens into another bed, so this is an ideal room for a family. Like the rest of the house, the master suite is furnished with antiques and family mementos such as the framed photo of Ann's uncle, a pioneer doctor whose most infamous patient was Wyatt Earp. (Her uncle, supposedly, was the model for the doctor in the television show about the legendary lawman.) There is an adjoining bath.

The only other bath in the house is in the back wing with two more bedrooms and three small sitting rooms, one with an eye-catching Navaho wall hanging and a stone fireplace. Youngsters should have a great time in the second-story "lookout" room, which has a single bed, a commanding view of the wooded terrain, and hand-painted rafters decorated with multicolored flowers, the handiwork of a Swedish artist who resided there awhile. Young and old alike should also be intrigued by T. C. Brown's African trophies reclining in the narrow hallway between the party rooms and the back bedrooms.

Exploring inside and out will be fun at this wonderful retreat, surely one of the area's best-kept secrets. Take one of the foot trails in back, and perhaps you'll chance upon the rare yellow violets that distinguish the treasured nature preserve, also a haven to three kinds of oak trees (chinquapin, red oak, and bur). It's rare that these species flourish together, not to mention for five hundred years! This is one bed and breakfast you won't want to miss, and all are welcome, including children, pets, even smokers (outside, at least). Rates are negotiable for parties, by the way.

4 bedrooms, 2 baths
Exclusive
No restrictions

BBTS NO. 25

She may be retired, but she's not retiring, and this former home economics teacher loves to meet new people. That's why she has opened her modest, one-story brick home to bed and breakfast guests. "I am not Will Rogers, but I never met a person I didn't find interesting or whom I couldn't learn something from," says Mattie.

With this kind of philosophy, it's no wonder she is a genial hostess who prides herself on pampering guests who are given a cheese and cracker tray upon arrival and a gourmet breakfast. Her popovers and biscuits are something you shouldn't miss, and so is her cheese toast, made from her own special sourdough starter, which she always keeps on hand.

The royal treatment in this north Garland home includes eating at Mattie's oversized dining room table. Her guest rooms are comfortable and clean. One has a double bed, while the second is actually a sitting room that has a fold-out couch that makes into a double bed. There is one shared bath.

An avid reader, Mattie keeps current copies of magazines like *Changing Times* and *National Geographic* around for guests to enjoy, too. After teaching school for forty-three years, Mattie misses the children, so it's not surprising that youngsters of all ages are welcome, providing they are well behaved. Since she has a fenced yard, pets have a haven here.

Richardson Square Mall is only a few blocks away, but bargain hunters might enjoy shopping in the outlet stores in nearby McKinney. This home is also near Southfork.

2 bedrooms, 1 shared bath
Budget
No restrictions

BBTS NO. 26

*T*his hostess was an extra on one of
the first *Dallas* shows televised. If you like, she'll show you her pictures of
J. R., Bobby, Pam, and Digger taken at Southfork, which is only about five
miles from her unassuming Garland home. Sally and Jerry will also show you
mementos of their European and Canadian travels, such as two swords from
Spain. Displayed in the den, the swords are crisscrossed into a shield bear-
ing Jerry's family crest. He made the shield.

Since there are two guest rooms, this eclectic home is ideal for those traveling with children. In one room, which has a queen-sized bed, are several
antiques, such as a spinning wheel, a rocker more than a hundred years old,
and an old-timey Philco radio. Soft blue colors predominate. If you're tall or
like to stretch, the second room might be for you, for it has an extra-long bed
that belonged to Sally's six-foot son. With one wall padded in a light rose,
beige, and grey paisley fabric to match pillows, curtains, and bedspread, the
room has a designer look. The bathroom, which must be shared if both rooms
are needed, is down the hall.

Breakfast treats will vary, from fried apples to waffles or biscuits and
gravy, but the hospitality will always be the same—warm and genuine.

2 bedrooms, 1 bath
Budget
No smoking. No pets.

Granbury

BBTS NO. 27

You'll pass pastoral scenes and peanut fields to reach this isolated B&B on a bend in the Brazos River near Granbury. Though it is only about fourteen miles from the acclaimed turn-of-the-century town, the drive takes about twenty minutes because the country road is winding and partly unpaved. Blink and you might miss the dirt road leading down the hill to your destination. In the spring, bluebonnets and other wildflowers blanket the hillside, while the reds, golds, and rust of the leaves on the trees behind the house paint a picture of their own each fall. This is a secluded retreat for all seasons.

The house itself is modest, but it offers a quiet haven from hectic city life. Walking through the woods in back of the house and along the Brazos River, building sand castles along the riverbed, or lolling around on an inner tube when there is enough water are the simple pleasures here. You can even borrow the hosts' canoe. Deer and other animals are often visible from the patio, where you can sit and watch the show.

Making guests feel like part of the family is the key to this couple's success as B&B hosts, and they welcome young and old alike. Watch television at night with them in the rustic den with its rock floor, and breakfast together in the morning on homemade banana, cherry nut, or raisin bread. Wake up to a cup of coffee served in your room.

The iron double bed in the guest room has a hand-quilted spread appliqued with oak leaf clusters. Above a marble-topped washstand is a wreath made from grapevines growing in their own backyard. A folder of area attractions such as Dinosaur State Park, thirty minutes away on the Paluxy River near Glen Rose, and the historic courthouse square in Granbury is always on the dresser.

Situated about thirty-six miles south of Fort Worth, Granbury has a restored town square that was the first in Texas to be declared a historic site. The opera house, built in 1886, offers year-round entertainment on most weekends, while the famous Nutt House draws people from near and far to eat its family-style fare. A picturesque hamlet with a progressive spirit, Granbury has some surprisingly cosmopolitan fashion boutiques on the square, along with antique and craft shops. You'll enjoy browsing. Polly will help you plan excursions and for a slight fee will give guided tours. Literally believing in going the extra mile for her B&B guests, she'll even provide transportation to and from DFW Airport!

1 bedroom, 1 bath
Moderate
No smoking. No pets.

Hurst

BBTS NO. 28

*S*tep up, step down throughout this intriguing trilevel Spanish-style white stucco home in Hurst, which is only about ten minutes from downtown Fort Worth, providing it's not rush hour. Convenient also to the Mid-Cities attractions, this bed and breakfast winner has a captivating sunken conversation area, affectionately referred to as "the pit" by Jane and JoAnne.

Flanked several feet above by a formal dining room on one side and the rest of the den on the other, the pit has comfortable couches, a wood-burning arched fireplace, and an intricately designed wrought-iron banister around it. The entire effect is very dramatic. This is where you'll probably sit and share a bottle of wine—perhaps a few tales—with the congenial hosts, who have traveled extensively.

A gorgeous lead crystal punch bowl is proudly displayed in the center of the dining room, and rightly so, for it won first place in its category at the Texas State Fair in 1983. A corner curio cabinet contains several sets of beautiful hundred-year-old Limoges china that were made in France. Like the punch bowl and china, most of the antiques in the house belong to Jane, including an 1830s partners desk, so called because the drawers and shelves are identical in front and back. The desk is in the small formal living room, which is dominated by a life-sized painting of Jane's favorite cousin, a Bostonian considered one of the three most beautiful women in that city when her portrait was painted, around 1930. The living room is next to the entry foyer, which has Italian-style tile on the floor and an old spinning wheel by the door, along with imposing portraits of Jane's great-great-grandparents. The eclectically furnished home has an international flavor, with Portuguese wallpaper and Dutch light fixtures in some of the rooms.

The guest bedroom has an early 1800s rope bed, a double, with a dust ruffle and a matching chest of drawers that previously belonged to Jane's grandparents. An adjoining half bath has only a toilet and sink, so guests bathe in the main bathroom down the hall. It has a sunken tub of blue and white Mexican mosaic tile and a shower. Since the room is carpeted and has matching mosaic tile on the countertop, it is striking.

You're welcome to use the backyard heated spa, too, and the umbrella-covered patio table. You'll share the house, by the way, with a small Yorkie named Little Mister and a Himalayan cat called Socrates.

When possible, Jane and JoAnne make airport pickups (for a nominal fee) and give guided tours of Fort Worth's famous stockyards. You won't leave hungry, either, for a hearty Texas breakfast is served. The two long-time friends call their home "a zoo" because there is always so much going on. See for yourself!

1 bedroom, 1 bath
Moderate
No pets

BBTS NO. 29

*T*he second Hurst home is more conventional, but equally inviting, primarily because the hosts are so warm and hospitable. Avid world travelers (ask about their camel ride in Egypt), they especially look forward to more visitors from abroad. They will provide transportation to and from nearby DFW Airport or wherever desired, for a slight fee, of course.

Quilting, ceramics, sewing, and crocheting are a few of Blanche's hobbies, and evidence of her handiwork is everywhere. Handmade pot holders and a towel are given each guest as a memento.

One large guest room has twin beds, an old-fashioned pedal sewing machine, one of Blanche's colorful afghans, and a ceiling fan. The other has a double bed with handmade quilt and French Provincial furniture. As thoughtful as she is talented, Blanche leaves nuts, fruit, gum, and magazines in the rooms and a curling iron and hair dryer in the adjoining bath, which must be shared if both rooms are in use. A telephone is available in the hall.

You'll have fun examining old-timey pieces that the creative couple have cleverly recycled, such as the huge wooden bowl that her grandmother once used when mixing dough for bread and biscuits. Now it holds current magazines. Another conversation piece is a glass-covered cast-iron pot that was formerly a washbasin for laundering clothes during days gone by, another family treasure. World War II ration coupons are displayed in the pot.

In the entrance hall are bells collected in Morocco, Switzerland, and other travel highpoints. Ask to see the old schoolhouse bell that once called her parents in to class. Its clang is as true today as it was then. Wedgwood plates from Jersey Island, which is off the English coast, are prized travel mementos, too, but the hosts serve breakfast on them.

Speaking of breakfast, how do pancakes and sausage, beer biscuits, juice, and coffee sound? Eat away to your heart's content in the cheerful garden room, which overlooks the heated spa. Feel free to use the spa, too. Their house is your house while you're a guest.

2 bedrooms, 1 bath
Moderate
No pets

Irving

*T*his California-style contemporary home in Irving has a lot of pizzazz. It has personality with a capital P, from the elegant foyer to brick floors throughout to the way the house forms a U around a small courtyard in back. On one side of the courtyard is a glass-enclosed solarium with a sauna and whirlpool. There are gold-plated fixtures on the whirlpool, which is surrounded by hanging baskets and plants. Heated and air-conditioned for year-round use, the solarium has a ceiling fan. A table and chairs are in one corner, in case you'd like to eat breakfast or even work out here. Bamboo grows wild and in profusion, forming a natural fence around the entire yard.

Overlooking the courtyard, which has lawn furniture scattered around, is the kitchen. Eat your huevos rancheros or grits and eggs here if you wish. The most interesting feature in the kitchen is the two-sided fireplace, which faces the living room on the other side. An independent interior accessories designer who specializes in original prints and collectibles, the hostess has tastefully placed samples around the living room, which doubles as a gallery for clients and business associates. Victorian couches and tables blend in beautifully.

Admitting that she fell in love with the house as soon as she saw it several years ago, Shirley points out that the downstairs guest room has a private entrance and its own bath. It also has a double bed that is a foot longer than most, so you tall men should sleep well. The bed once belonged to her 6'7" father. A white quilt with red and pink roses made by her mother will keep you warm. A corner antique secretary/hutch is made to order for the busy executive, while an Italian imported brass lamp is interesting.

Watch your head going up the narrow stairs to the guest room above. If you want privacy, you've certainly got it here! What fun, too, for you must climb up two giant steps into the platform bed, which has a good, firm mattress. It sleeps two. A bathtub and so forth are across the room, with a chest-high wall providing a bit of privacy.

You Cowboy fans ought to check out this B&B, because it is close to Texas Stadium. It's also near DFW Airport and the Las Colinas business complex. Twenty minutes or so (depending on the traffic) and you're in downtown Dallas, too.

2 bedrooms, 2 baths
Moderate
No smoking. No children.
No pets

Jefferson

Staying in a bed and breakfast
home is even more memorable than usual in Jefferson, where most of the
historic homes now open to overnight guests are beautifully furnished with
period pieces. Few people would question that with its restored homes and
famed Excelsior Hotel Jefferson is becoming known as one of the most important bed and breakfast towns in Texas. Because of its popularity for weekend
jaunts, it's wise to make reservations for a bed and breakfast home in Jefferson as far in advance as possible.

Jefferson has an interesting history. Situated at the intersection of U.S.
Highways 49 and 59 about three hours from Dallas, this East Texas town was
once the largest inland shipping port in the state. It was established in 1836
and enjoyed a twenty-year boom as a major river port. At the time, Big Cypress Bayou was navigable, and as many as fifteen palatial steamboats were
often lined up at the docks. When the Corps of Engineers blasted a logjam on
Caddo Lake nearby, the bayou became navigable only by smaller boats, and
Jefferson's prosperity faded. During its heyday the population had soared to
30,000, but later the populace dwindled rapidly.

Railroad tycoon Jay Gould thought that Jefferson's future lay with rail, and he supposedly came to town in 1882 to get approval to lay down tracks. He was turned down. One generation has passed along to another the story that Gould angrily predicted the end of Jefferson in the Excelsior Hotel register as he checked out, telling those within earshot that "grass would grow in the streets and bats would roost in the belfries." Whether he actually said these things has been disputed in recent years, but his dire predictions nevertheless almost came true. Jefferson was a dying town for many years, until the ladies of the Jessie Allen Wise Garden Club bought the Excelsior Hotel and restored it to its present grandeur with marble-topped dressers, armoires, and other fine antique pieces. Its restoration prompted a citywide effort to recapture Jefferson's past, and tourism has brought prosperity once again.

Be sure to take one of the guided tours of the Excelsior and treat yourself to the fabled Plantation breakfast, which includes orange-blossom muffins, mayahaw jelly, and more, for $4.50. Reservations must be made in advance. The renowned Jefferson Historical Museum is just opposite the Excelsior and boasts more than three thousand priceless artifacts.

Another restored hostelry worth exploring is the New Jefferson Inn, also near the Excelsior on Austin Street. Built in 1861 as a huge warehouse in which to store cotton bales awaiting shipment downriver, it was converted to a hotel around the turn of the century. It has twenty-two rooms with marvelous antiques and a restaurant that offers meals at very reasonable prices.

Speaking of food, Jefferson is a gourmet delight, with the Black Swan, the Stillwater Inn, and the Galley Pub all offering great cuisine and incredible ambience. The Bakery, the Ice Cream Emporium, and the Mint Tulip Coffee Saloon are must stops, too, along with Auntie Skinner's Riverboat Club nearby. For a quiet town, Jefferson has a lot going for it that will make you want to come back time and again, especially when you tour the magnificent historic homes like the Magnolias, the House of the Seasons, and those open to bed and breakfast lodgers. Wander around the waterfront and the antique shops, take a horse-drawn carriage or scenic boat-ride tour, or rent a paddle-wheel boat or a bicycle—the opportunities for adventure in Jefferson are almost endless.

Jefferson is a wonderful place to visit any time of the year. However, the annual spring pilgrimage in May, the Marion County fair each fall (which includes an arts and crafts fair and a syrup-soppin' contest), and a beautiful Christmas Candlelight Tour are special times for this special town. Jefferson is also a great base for visits to nearby Caddo Lake and Lake o' the Pines, not to mention the races in Louisiana.

For more information on Jefferson's attractions, contact the Chamber of

Commerce, 116 W. Austin, Jefferson 75657. And don't forget to make a reservation as far in advance as possible to stay at one of the marvelous bed and
breakfast inns, which will help make your trek to Jefferson seem even more
like a trip back in time.

AUSTIN COTTAGE

*M*ost anyone in Jefferson can direct you to "the little red house standing on the hill." The natty frame house
is called Austin Cottage, which is appropriate since it is located at 406 Austin, just a few blocks from the Excelsior. Built around 1891, Austin Cottage
is one of the few remaining board and batten houses in Jefferson. (Houses of
this type had batten—small strips of wood—put between the boards, primarily to keep cold air from coming in.)

The cozy cottage belongs to Cindy Edwards, who lives there herself when
she doesn't have bed and breakfast guests. She leaves a lengthy welcome
note for guests, telling a little about herself (she writes for the Marshall newspaper) and a lot about the cottage, which she hopes they'll love as much as
she does. Cindy also leaves croissants, coffee, and juice so they can help
themselves to a continental breakfast in the morning. The country kitchen
has no doors on the cabinets; antique china and chickens—collectibles that
had been her mother's—are displayed on the top of the cabinets.

Furnished with antiques handed down to the young homeowner by her beloved grandmother, Austin Cottage has a surprisingly chic decor, with wonderful French doors, wooden shutters adorned with fabric, striking window
treatments, and some modern touches: central air and heat, even a television. Shades of blue, Cindy's favorite color, appear throughout the charming
guest house except in the bedroom, which is a pale pink. The comforter on
the old-timey white pine double bed matches the Oriental cotton print draped
across one wall. The claw-foot tub in the adjoining bathroom has been converted into a shower as well.

Relax on the overstuffed couch in the spacious living room or enjoy the sun room, which was added a few years after the house was constructed. The blue and white wicker rocker, sofa, and chair had also belonged to her grandparents, and Cindy remembers how her grandmother always told her grandfather, "You're going to wear that old rocker out." But the rocker has endured, just like the little red house on the hill. Smokers are welcome, and so are children thirteen and older.

Cindy Edwards
406 Austin
Jefferson 75657
(214) 665-8955
1 bedroom, 1 bath
Exclusive
No children under 13. No pets.

COLLINS HOUSE

*T*he two-story white frame farmhouse—looking bed and breakfast inn that sprawls across a large corner lot at 409 S. Alley seems a little out of place in a town touted for its Victorian gems. Built from cypress wood, the Collins House is the only early Texas—style home in Jefferson. Indications are that it was built between 1888 and 1896 by a Mr. Minnter, a lumberman who bought the lot from Dan Alley. No one knows just why Mr. Minnter chose this style, but the house was obviously designed for comfort and family living, since it has eight bedrooms (four on each floor) and a big seventy-foot wraparound rock porch. Narrow pillars all around the porch give it added pizzazz. Guests love to eat breakfast on the porch or unwind in the swing or rocking chairs at night, perhaps with a glass of wine. You probably will, too.

The country look is carried out inside, although antiques are in the spacious rooms as well. Twelve-foot-high ceilings, French doors between the formal living and dining rooms, and bay windows designed to catch the breeze are a few of the noteworthy features of this fine house. Air-conditioned in the

Collins House

1920s, the house also has ceiling fans, added for charm as well as comfort by Sue Collins, who acquired it about four years ago.

Since there are more than three thousand square feet of space and thirteen rooms on the first floor alone, Sue uses the upstairs only for storage. Three of the four downstairs bedrooms are for bed and breakfast guests. To the left of the main entrance is a country suite with a sitting area, a kitchenette, and a double bed. A washstand, pitcher, and bowl add a Victorian touch. A bath is shared with the adjoining Rose Room, so the two rooms would be perfect for a family or two couples. Chintz curtains carry out the country look in the spacious Rose Room, which has an antique brass double bed with a hand-made quilt, and another washstand, pitcher, and bowl. There are a number of other interesting antiques in this elegant room, including a clock and a windup telephone. Called the Blue Room, the third bedroom has a four-poster double bed, an antique oak chest, and a private bath, probably added in the 1920s. All three rooms have private entrances.

Each room also has its own coffee pot so guests can make coffee, hot chocolate, or hot cider whenever they wish. Apple strudel, orange juice, and fruit in season are brought to the rooms between 8 and 8:30 in the morning. If you want directions to any of the attractions or places of interest in Jefferson, just ask Sue, who keeps tourist information on hand along with menus from the restaurants. The accommodating public relations specialist welcomes young and old, even small pets like poodles, to the Collins House. The guest rooms have all the comforts you'll need, but no telephones or televisions. Who would want to watch television when she could sit on the big front porch and rock?

Sue Collins
409 S. Alley
Jefferson 75657
(214) 665-2483
3 bedrooms, 2 baths
Moderate
No restrictions

THE COTTAGE IN
JEFFERSON

*F*eatured on the Christmas Candle-
light Tour recently, the Cottage in Jefferson is a bed and breakfast inn only on
weekends, and a carefully supervised nutritional weight-loss center during
the week, believe it or not. Located at 307 Soda, the salmon-colored three-
level Victorian house has a lot of gingerbread, a white picket fence, and furnishings that could have been found in a similar house in the late 1800s
when it was constructed. B. J. Terry bought the land in 1865, then built the
quaint cottage for a daughter. Emma lived there until 1900, when she sold it
to a family who kept it for forty-three years. Subsequently possessed by several others, it finally was acquired by two East Texas women as an investment
in 1982. Peggy Porter Boyland and Nelda Sullivan Milam spent the following
year renovating their find, doing much of the work themselves although nei-
ther had ever papered, painted, or put in windows before. Knocking down a
brick wall that had been erected around the porch during the 1930s was a
monumental task that they didn't attempt themselves, however. After com-
pleting the restoration, they spent two months shopping for just the right
antiques.

Justifiably pleased with the results, the two point out that the cottage can
accommodate as many as sixteen people because there are trundle beds in
each of the four bedrooms. The cottage can be rented for a night by individuals or by a group. (Group rates are available.)

Not only the furniture, but also the paintings, prints, and tapestry wall
hangings are antiques as well. Even the cups used for tea are from an antique
Victorian collection purchased from an estate. There are a number of interesting pieces, including a pegged table in the entry, a gateleg tea table edged
with lovely hand carvings, an American Empire sofa, and a porcelain and
bronze lamp on a skirted table in the parlor.

The Rose Room on the first floor to the right of the entrance has a king-sized bedroom suite that was made in Germany almost eighty years ago. It is the only furniture in the house that isn't Victorian. Adjoining this striking room is a bath with a claw-foot tub. Also on the first floor is a tiny day room with a spindle bed, if you only need a single. On the first landing upstairs is an airy sun room with a queen-sized bed and wicker furniture. Go up some more stairs to the left and you're in a spacious blue room with a four-poster iron and brass double bed, an oak dresser, and two chairs in a seating area. The charming bed and breakfast room even has a dressing area in an alcove. Wildflower wallpaper gives the final guest room its name, the Wildflower Room. It has a double bed and an antique quilt. The latter three rooms share a bath.

Although the owners don't live in the cottage themselves as most bed and breakfast innkeepers do, they have someone special who will cater to your needs. Breakfast, which includes hot apricot or apple strudel from the Bakery, as well as juice and coffee, will be served at 8 A.M. You can eat in the formal dining room or on a tray in your room. The big kitchen has an ice-maker, a coffee pot, and other necessities, so you can fix anything else you'd like.

Don't forget that reservations are accepted only for weekends. If you'd like to lose weight while having a good time, check further on the cottage's weight-loss program, which includes three meals a day (you'll want the recipes), twice-a-day exercise, and entertainment. You'll tour historic homes and churches, antique shops and museums during the day and play bridge, Trivial Pursuit, or whatever at night. A midweek highlight is a trip to Auntie Skinner's Riverboat Club. The Cottage in Jefferson is about two and a half blocks from the heart of the historic district.

Be sure to sign the guest book in the parlor!

307 Soda
Jefferson 75657
(214) 665-8572
4 bedrooms, 2 baths
Moderate
No children. No pets.

THE GUEST HOUSE

*I*nstead of hand-carved wood and hundred-year-old furniture, you'll find a more casual yet equally charming decor in the Guest House. Rustic willow furniture fills both bedrooms as well as the living room, and it's very appealing. Karen Capers, who owns the Guest House, is so sold on willow furniture, incidentally, that she sells it now on the second floor of a well-known restaurant, the Black Swan (formerly Ruthmary's). Located on the edge of the historic district, the Guest House is a one-story frame house that has a smoke-blue exterior with Berber ivory trim and a bright red door. Built around 1920, the small house is constructed a few feet off the ground on pier beams.

You'll really recapture the past in this unusual bed and breakfast inn because it has a 1936 Magic Chef range—in perfect working order—and an old-fashioned ice box, complete with a block of ice. Karen leaves heart-shaped bread for B&B guests. The bread might be banana nut, apricot, walnut, or pumpkin, and all of it is good! Hot cinnamon bread is another possibility, along with hot spiced cider, hot cocoa, and coffee. Intent on helping honeymooners enjoy their stay, the thoughtful hostess also leaves wine or champagne for them.

Though the Guest House can accommodate six, it is rented to only one couple at a time unless the group is together. Since a doghouse is out back, you can even bring your pet. Furnished free along with the Guest House is a bicycle built for two. You might enjoy biking around the small town. Then you can relax at night on the swing in back of the Guest House, at least when the weather is pleasant.

511 W. Austin
Jefferson 75657
(214) 665-8774
2 bedrooms, 1 bath
Exclusive
No restrictions

HALE HOUSE

Some say Linda Leonard serves the best breakfast in Jefferson at the Hale House, which overlooks the city park. Guests can have omelets, quiche, or pancakes for breakfast, along with cheese grits and homemade pastries. Linda is following in the footsteps of May Belle Hale, who lived in her family's home for many, many years. Reportedly an excellent cook, too, May Belle probably had the happiest boarders in town. She turned the family home into a boarding house in the 1920s after enlarging it to its present size. A Greek Revival structure, it consisted only of four rooms and a central hall on one floor when it was built in 1865. The house is considerably larger now, with five beautifully furnished guest rooms in a second story, and the section added by May Belle can easily be detected because the siding boards are narrower than on the oiginal part of the house. May Belle Hale was quite a gal, by the way. Not only was she the most noted music teacher and civic leader in Jefferson for many a day, but she is said to have conducted three symphony orchestras at the same time. That sounds like quite a feat, especially for those days of old.

With the magnificent magnolia tree, white pillars, and American flag flying in front, the Hale House is very striking. Linda and Mark Leonard acquired the stately bed and breakfast inn about two years ago from the former owner, who had opened it to overnight guests in 1981. The interior decor is just as beautiful as its exterior. The most interesting feature of the formal living room to the left of the entrance is that the wallpaper is a replica of paper in the Ford Theater when Lincoln was shot. A deep burgundy with a small floral pattern and striped effect, the subdued paper complements the period furniture and hardwood floors nicely.

Across the hall is a smaller parlor, part of the master suite. Occasionally you'll see a little girl's frilly dress hanging on the doorknob, waiting for a customer. A talented seamstress, Linda custom-makes clothes for little girls.

Besides a big, functional kitchen, the first floor includes a formal dining room with a Duncan Phyfe reproduction table and Chippendale chairs. On the wall hangs a blue and red floral quilt with incredibly small stitches that say "Rebecca McCoy, May 22, 1839." Rebecca was one of Linda's ancestors. You can eat breakfast here or on the more informal sun porch, which has hanging baskets and wicker furniture. A lot of the Leonards's B&B guests like to read the newspaper or maybe even play a game of cards out here at night. For the convenience of guests, a bucket and an icemaker are always available. Breakfast is usually served between 8 and 9:30, although early risers can have their first cup of coffee at 6:30, when it's placed on an oak sideboard in the upstairs hall.

The five guest rooms are all very comfortable and inviting, with different color schemes: blue, peach, pink, rose, and lilac. The blue and peach rooms share a bath, which has a big claw-foot tub; the rest have private baths. While the rose and lilac rooms have queen-sized beds, the other three all have double beds. All rooms but the rose have rockers. There is a white wicker cradle in the blue room and a baby bed in the pink room. Although officially accepting only nonsmoking overnight guests, the Leonards say that smoking might occasionally be permitted outside or on the porch.

You'll find literature on Jefferson in the upstairs hall, and Linda will be happy to help plan your stay in this historic town. If you don't feel like walking around, borrow the hosts' ten-speed or tandem bikes.

Mark and Linda Leonard,
innkeepers
702 S. Line
Jefferson 75657
(214) 665-8877
5 rooms, 4 baths
Moderate
No smoking. No pets.

HORN'S GINGERBREAD HOUSE

*C*ome spend one night or seven in the antique-filled home of Douglas and Norma Horn or in the guest house in back. Formerly their garage apartment, Horn's Gingerbread House includes two bedrooms, a nice-sized living room, a dining room, and a kitchen. Despite its name, it is not as ornate or as sumptuously furnished as some of the other Victorian bed and breakfast inns, including the Horn home itself; but the Gingerbread House has its own brand of charm and is very private. Even if you need just one room, the entire place will be yours, and for a very reasonable price. Since there is a hide-a-bed, six can be accommodated here.

Horn's Gingerbread House has an antique oak double bed in one bedroom and twin beds in the other. Modernized for your comfort, it has air-conditioning and heat and a television. A round oak pedestal table and antique buffet are among interesting pieces. The kitchen is fully equipped, so you can fix some of your meals here if you can resist the delicious cuisine available in local restaurants.

Norma, who specializes in silk flower arrangements and catering, prepares delicious breakfast goodies for her guests, whether they eat in the Gingerbread House or her home. Bacon bites, gingerbread muffins, and a gorgeous fruit salad are traditional fare. Surprising guests with something extra like tiny chicken salad sandwiches for a late-night snack is not unusual for Norma. Served on her best china and crystal on an antique golden oak clawfoot table in the dining room, breakfast is elegant indeed.

Crammed full of fabulous antique pieces and family heirlooms, the dining room has a showpiece: a dazzling nine-by-nine-foot china cabinet. Norma swapped a nine-piece dining room set for this massive marvel. In the crowded living room are other Victorian gems, including a gold loveseat and an oak sideboard. The Horns cherish an antique clock with beveled glass that their son sent them from the Black Forest in Germany.

Just wait until you see the guest bedroom! The early Victorian walnut double bed has an eight-foot-tall ornately carved headboard that matches a marble-topped dresser. Both belonged to her husband's grandmother and look very impressive. A platform rocker is interesting. The bedroom has an adjoining bath.

Although smoking is not permitted in the house, which was built in 1916, you can smoke in the Gingerbread House. Pets may also stay in the guest house.

**Douglas and Norma Horn,
innkeepers
601 E. Jefferson
Jefferson 75657
(214) 665-8994
3 bedrooms, 2 baths
Moderate
Smoking only in the guest house
Pets only in the guest house**

PRIDE HOUSE

*J*efferson's pride and joy—or one of them, anyway—is the Pride House, a magnificent gabled mansion with stained-glass windows in every room. Painted a rich caramel color with white gingerbread trim and sky-blue accents, it sits imposingly on the corner of its block. Towering over one side of the house is an ancient pecan tree with a swing hanging from one of its highest branches. The Pride House has a big wraparound porch where you can relax in antique rocking chairs and perhaps reflect on what it might have been like living here when Jefferson was a bustling river port. Closer inspection will reveal superb craftsmanship, the original ornate bronze hardware on heavy, five-paneled doors, and a Texas Historical Marker.

One of the first bed and breakfast inns in Texas, the Pride House is becoming one of the most popular, partly because of its ambience and partly because of innkeeper Ruthmary Jordan's gracious hospitality. Built in 1888 by lumberman George Brown from a mail-order blueprint, the grand old house was damaged by a fire about fifteen years ago. Vacant and deteriorating, it looked almost haunted. It was overgrown with shrubs and cobwebs and had peeling paint, rotting boards, and a fallen porch—a far cry from the house that was considered one of Jefferson's finest at the turn of the century. Falling in love with the house despite its decay, Ruthmary's daughter, Sandy Spalding, and her husband bought and restored it. It's named for their son, Pride. When the family moved to Oregon, Ruthmary became the innkeeper.

The Pride House has four captivating guest rooms, each with its own quaint private bath, telephone, and period decor, including armoires instead of closets for your clothes. One bedroom has a wood-burning fireplace that will make your room even cozier. Oversized beds, eyelet pillow shams and dust ruffles, wonderful wallpaper, wicker, and brass lamps add to the atmosphere. At night, open the blinds so the morning sunlight can stream in through the gorgeous stained-glass windows. It's a delightful way to awaken!

There are four more rooms with private baths in the guest house out back called the Dependency, which looks like a life-sized dollhouse. Originally built as a two-room cottage for servants, it now has two more rooms that were added recently to help cope with the increasing demand from bed and breakfast travelers. The two-story addition looks just like the original, so its character has been maintained. While the Dependency's old rooms have Victorian decors, the two new ones include more country primitive pieces. A

Pride House

wood-burning fireplace in the added downstairs suite and a balcony porch on the upper make both very inviting. All four suites have access to a common kitchen, which has some old-timey touches like a wooden drainboard and old-fashioned flour bin, along with modern conveniences. Since a hideaway bed can be put in front of the fireplace, the Dependency can actually accommodate up to nine, and children are welcome here but not in the Pride House itself.

The hostelry is becoming noted for its gourmet breakfasts, which is understandable since Ruthmary formerly owned a highly acclaimed restaurant (Ruthmary's, now the Black Swan). Bran muffins with a hint of almond, bread pudding topped with praline sauce, poached pears in cream, orange butter, and Cajun coffee are among the tantalizing treats, all elegantly served in crystal. Fill your tray from an enormous old wardrobe now used as a central food receiver for guests in the upper hallway, then breakfast in the privacy of your room or even on the front porch.

Take time to explore the house, which has furnishings from other periods as well as Victorian. From the carved oak mantel in the parlor to a desk dating back to the Revolutionary War, from its twelve-foot-high ceilings to the nine-foot windows, the Pride House is something special. So is Ruthmary Jordan. Find out for yourself why Jeffersonians take so much pride in them.

409 E. Broadway
Jefferson 75657
(214) 665-2675
8 bedrooms, 8 baths
Moderate to exclusive
No pets

WILLIAM CLARK HOUSE

*F*or more than forty-three years, this peach-colored gabled home was owned by the family of William Clark, a leading citizen who served as postmaster as well as judge. With its white picket fence, small front porch, and Victorian millwork, the picturesque house looks much the same today as it did then. Although the fence had been torn down some time ago, it was replaced by Suzanne Benefield, who has owned the house for the past few years, to restore it to its look of old.

Located in the heart of the historic district, the bed and breakfast inn not only boasts a Texas historical medallion but is listed in the National Register of Historic Places as well. The date on the medallion is 1852, the year the first two rooms were built by Allen Urquhart, who cofounded Jefferson with Dan Alley. The remaining rooms were added subsequently.

Just around the corner from the Excelsior, the William Clark House has one guest room, and the little cottage in back has two more. In Victorian times, mattresses were often placed on top of rope strung across the frame in lieu of box springs, and one of these rope beds is probably the most significant antique in the front bedroom of the house. The walnut four-poster is a double. A Victorian strip carpet with a pink and rose floral pattern enhances the room, which also includes a handcrafted Victorian rocker and a marble-topped washstand.

Even more intriguing is the huge connecting bath with its oversized cast-iron tub lined with porcelain, an antique washstand, and a double-mirrored armoire. In a nod to Victorian modesty, the water closet is hidden. At various times through the years the space was used as a bedroom and even a kitchen.

The rest of the William Clark House is charming, too, including the present kitchen, with its extremely large 1920s Garland stove, and the living room, which has a parlor grand piano and what looks like a coal-burning fireplace that now burns gas. A Duncan Phyfe table, an antique mirror, and Swiss lace curtains will catch your eye in the dining room.

Though rollaway cots are available for any of the rooms, Suzanne usually tells guests they will probably be more comfortable in the little cottage behind the house if they have children. Both rooms have separate entries and private baths. The first has a Pennsylvania Dutch double bed with a floral pattern on the headboard and footboard. The yellow bed, a golden oak table, and a marble-topped chest are described as "a poor man's Victorian furniture" by Suzanne, who is director of the House of the Seasons, which can be toured daily. She's named this room the Gold Room. The second room in the cottage has twin beds, walnut period reproduction furniture, and plenty of space, too. There are ancient pecan trees all around the backyard, which you'll see as you go in and out of the cottage.

Whether you stay in the William Clark House or in the cottage, you'll eat breakfast in the formal dining room. Baked apples, raisin-bran muffins, and mixed fruit in season are among the offerings.

201 W. Henderson
Jefferson 75657
(214) 665-8880
3 bedrooms, 3 baths
Moderate
No pets

WISE MANOR

*T*ownspeople say that if you want to know something about Jefferson, you should just ask Katherine Ramsay Wise. This well-known historian, who was voted the outstanding citizen of the year, has one of the best bed and breakfast inns in town. Wise Manor is a captivating two-story salmon-colored cottage with white gingerbread trim, a gabled roof, a small porch, and a white wrought-iron fence. Shaded by tall pecan trees, it has a Texas Historical Marker. Members of Katherine's family have lived in the house for more than sixty years, and in Jefferson even longer, so family treasures fill every room.

Like many of the houses in Jefferson, this was only a two-room structure when it was built in 1851. The other rooms were added around 1874, and Katherine's family made further changes in the 1920s. The picturesque cottage is now in a quiet residential area, but long ago this was a very busy and exciting part of Jefferson, with many horses and buggies and wagons passing

Wise Manor on the way into town from the Big Cypress Ferry a few blocks away. The road in front of the cottage was the main entry into Jefferson. During Reconstruction, southerners rebelling against Yankee control were imprisoned in a stockade nearby, so this is a historic area as well.

Wise Manor has three extra-special guest rooms. The downstairs bedroom furniture, including a double bed, dates back to the 1930s. The adjoining private bath has a small claw-foot tub and shower. "Primitive country" best describes the blue room upstairs, which has a handmade pine rope bed that in olden days held a cornshuck mattress, bookshelves made from a chicken crate, and a pine bench from one of the earliest log cabins in Marion County. It's very homey. In fact, Katherine teases, "Everybody staying in this room says it's like coming home to Grandma's." You coffee drinkers will be happy to know that a coffee pot is in one corner of the room, so you can make yourself a cup whenever you wish.

The blue room shares a bath with a more elegant room with a dusty rose decor, so Katherine rents only one room at a time unless both are needed by a family or two couples traveling together. The dusty rose room has some wonderful Victorian furniture, including a walnut Mallard bed. The signature of this noted New Orleans furnituremaker—an egg—is carved at the top of the huge walnut headboard. Another very special bed is in the adjoining alcove. Most Victorian beds are doubles, but this custom-made youth bed is a single, which makes it rather unique. It too has a high headboard. There are a telephone and television in this beautiful room, but guests are also welcome to watch TV in the parlor.

"Manageable" children are invited to enjoy the hospitality of Wise Manor, which is now air-conditioned. Since so many visitors like to eat the famous Plantation breakfast at the Excelsior, Mrs. Wise is happy to make arrangements for her guests at the Excelsior. For an extra fee, she will prepare a continental breakfast if it is requested.

312 Houston
Jefferson 75657
(214) 665-2386
3 bedrooms, 2 baths
Moderate
No pets

Lake Ray Hubbard

BBTS NO. 31

*M*other Nature puts on quite a show at this Lake Ray Hubbard haven, from the waves of migrating monarch butterflies that cling to the trees each April and fall to the vibrant red spider lilies in mid-October. In the spring there are sweet-scented jonquils and hyacinths. More than sixty pecan trees dot the property, and you can watch the squirrels at play from the patio in back, which also overlooks a creek. Only the hootey-hoot-hoot of owls occasionally breaks the silence at this rustic retreat, which is about thirty minutes from downtown Dallas.

The sparkling waters of Lake Ray Hubbard glisten through the trees, promising exciting recreational adventures. A large man-made reservoir, Lake Ray Hubbard has great fishing and boating facilities, while year-round excursions are available on the recently renovated riverboat, the Texas Queen, each Saturday at 11 A.M. and 12:30, along with dinner cruises

Wednesday and Sunday evenings. Taking in the championship rodeo in nearby Mesquite, held each Friday and Saturday April through September, is another possibility for those who stay in this captivating B&B.

The hostess will be happy to help arrange reservations for any of these activities, unless you prefer just to enjoy the serenity of her quiet home, which she shares with a Persian cat named Smokey, and with Mitzy, her Lhasa apso. Jeanne's unusual elongated two-story home has a steep sloping roof, vaulted ceilings, exposed beams, and parquet floors. Since blue is her favorite color, there are accents of it throughout, including a blue floral chintz sofa in the paneled den and an overstuffed hundred-year-old blue rocker in the living room. A sliding glass door leads to the patio.

The larger of two guest bedrooms is not blue, but a sunny yellow. Even the king-sized bed has a yellow finish. Watch television in bed if you wish, for a portable color TV in the den can easily be moved into the bedroom. The second guest room has twin beds. Seeing to her guests' comfort is important to Jeanne, who usually serves blueberry muffins, eggs and bacon, fruit or juice, and coffee. On nice days, you might want to eat on the patio or just sit out there at night and enjoy the outdoors. Small pets are welcome here.

2 bedrooms, 2 baths
Moderate
No restrictions

Plano

BBTS NO. 32

*Y*ou'll find flowers year-round in the secluded yard at this comfortable Plano home, which is only a few miles from Southfork. This growing suburb, about ten miles from Dallas, has also gained fame as the hot air balloon capital of Texas. The Plano-Coors Hot Air Balloon Festival, held the last weekend in September, draws balloonists from all over the world and more than ten thousand spectators. You can see these colorful balloons floating gently over Plano most weekends of the year, usually just before sunset or right after sunrise.

If you're a hot air balloon buff, you might enjoy staying at this B&B, which is in an exclusive country club addition. Tennis courts, a golf course, and other facilities at the club make this home attractive for any sportsminded guest, not just those who have business in the area. Literature about the entire Dallas–Fort Worth area is always on hand in the guest rooms. Dorothy and Don will help guests make reservations for dinner.

The hosts have two guest rooms available. The first has lovely antique cherry furniture with a double bed and a private bath. An Amish bedroom scene on the wall has special meaning. Purchased while Dorothy and Don were vacationing in the Smokies, the picture shows a blue and white quilt on a bed. When they got to New York, Dorothy showed the picture to a ninety-three-year-old woman who has made quilts for other members of her family through the years, and the oldtimer is making a quilt for Dorothy just like the one in the picture.

The second bedroom has twin beds with white ruffled spreads. A doll collection that had belonged to the couple's daughters, Judi and Melodie, are in a cradle and a piano bench. The two rooms share the bath when both are in use.

If you forget your toothbrush or comb, don't worry, for the grandmotherly hostess keeps a basket of toiletries in the bathroom just for you. Writing paper, pens, stamps, and wrapping paper are also provided as another thoughtful touch.

A coffeemaker and portable oven are available for your room if you prefer fixing your own breakfast, but most guests enjoy eating with the hosts in the cozy breakfast nook. As you devour homemade sweet rolls and biscuits, sausage and eggs, look out the window and watch the hummingbirds flirt with the feeder. A carrot cake or some other tempting dessert will usually be in the oven or on the counter in the homey kitchen, because the hostess loves to bake. "Baking makes a house smell like a home," she says. Like many other B&B hostesses, Dorothy will provide transportation to and from the airport and around town.

2 bedrooms, 1 bath
Moderate
No smoking. No pets.

Royse City

*I*f you like to soar or just enjoy watching others glide through the air, consider staying at this splendid Victorian home in Royse City. It's about ten minutes from Caddo Mills, a center for soaring activities, primarily in summer and fall. (National competition is held there.)

Royse City is a rather nondescript community without even a courthouse square. But the features that make this such a special stopover for even those who have business in Dallas are the hospitality of the hosts (he's the mayor and a junior high coach and she's a talented artist and teacher) and the charm of the house itself.

A Rockwall County Historical Marker indicates the significance of this impressive white frame house, probably the nicest in town with its big columns, second-floor balcony, hand-carved front door adorned with oval-shaped beveled glass, and a white picket fence. Shaded by two enormous cedar trees, it sits majestically on the corner, not too many blocks from Interstate Highway 30. The first story was built in 1897 by a prosperous banker as a wedding present for his daughter; the second was added a few years later.

The gregarious hosts, who acquired their dream house in 1980, have blended family heirlooms and more modern pieces for an understated elegance, especially in the living room, which is enhanced by greenery galore. A crystal chandelier and an imposing portrait of Sharon's grandmother in the formal dining room draw your eye. You can breakfast here, but most prefer to sample Sharon's wonderful waffles and western omelets (and strawberries from their garden in season) in the country kitchen. It's crammed with collectibles, such as cherished tin boxes and painted plaques and other handiwork done by the hostess. There is also a nifty reproduction of an antique highchair, which can be converted into a rocker for tiny tots.

A winding staircase leads to the upstairs guest quarters, which include a private bath, a sitting room with a television set, and a cheerful green and yellow bedroom. The latter has four-poster twin beds that belonged to Sharon's great-grandparents and an antique cradle similar to one found in the Ford Museum. You can even have breakfast on the adjoining balcony while you listen to the birds chirping away. The accommodating couple offer their own king-sized bed downstairs to honeymooners and those observing special occasions.

1 bedroom, 1 bath
Moderate
No smoking. No pets.

Waco

BBTS NO. 34

W hile in Dallas to attend the El Greco exhibit at the Museum of Fine Arts, Rosemary and Bob stayed in a B&B. Because they enjoyed the experience so much, they subsequently became B&B hosts themselves. Fortunately so, for their lakeside home is special indeed. The sprawling split-level home backs up to a lake, while a country club, complete with golf course, is only a few doors down. A long redwood deck parallels the back of the house and overlooks the lake. There is a basket swing on the wooden deck and a hammock by the water, so relaxing is in order. Fishing is, too, if your interests run that way.

Located about fifteen minutes from the center of town, this is an ideal B&B for those who are flying in and out of the airport or visiting offspring attending nearby Baylor University. (An Arizona couple stayed there while enrolling their son at Baylor, and he often studies at their spacious home on weekends to get away from the crowded dorm. In fact, he's become their "adopted" son.)

Even though Rosemary teaches business at a local high school, she graciously volunteers to take guests around to see the old suspension bridge, the zoo, nearby Bentwood Farms (home for several thousand rare Egyptian Arabian horses, one valued at $10 million), and other Waco attractions. There is a slight charge for this service.

The Olympic-sized pool, tennis courts, and other facilities at the country club will be at your disposal, even for dinner. Bob is always looking for a golf partner, so bring your clubs.

Rosemary is a gourmet cook and prepares crepes or omelets on weekends. She serves a continental breakfast during the week, since she and her husband leave early for work. However, the kitchen is yours to fix anything else you'd like. When the weather is pretty, you can breakfast on the deck.

Since they have a dog pen, their hospitality even extends to pets. The elegance of the house is echoed in the guest room, by the way. The cozy first-floor bedroom has a double bed, a ceiling fan, and a picture of a duck on the wall. There is a shared bath.

1 bedroom, 1 shared bath
Moderate
No restrictions

BBTS NO. 35

*T*he hostess does oil and china painting, makes fantastic cakes for weddings and special occasions, sews like a professional, embroiders beautifully, gives pastry-making demonstrations to garden clubs, and has a green thumb and a warm heart. It's no wonder that this lovely lady and her equally talented husband (his specialties are woodworking and stained glass) make marvelous B&B hosts.

Their rambling, two-story home on the south side of town reflects their varied talents, from the towering vine shooting up the wall to the vaulted ceiling in the foyer to the stained-glass panel of his family crest in the hall. Many of her fabulous oils glorify the majestic Alps in their native Germany. Although they came to this country almost thirty years ago, the hospitable couple retain their European charm.

You'll immediately feel at home with them, chatting in the comfortable den or kitchen, in the garden room, or, weather permitting, on the patio. Breakfast can be taken anywhere you like and usually consists of bacon or sausage, eggs, juice, and coffee. The hostess loves to bake, and her homemade fruit pastries will prove irresistible. Don't count the calories. Just enjoy!

The pink and white guest room is very feminine. Umpteen pillows, predominantly pink and white, some with green stitching, look fetching on the double bed, which has a white spread. The pretty pillows were designed and made by Hildegarde and her teenage daughter. The two also collaborated on the multicolored floral hooked rug in the hall. You'll have a private bath, by the way. If two couples or a family need a second room, one is available.

If you like to fish, you'll be interested to know that a lake is almost within walking distance of this exclusive neighborhood. Fort Fisher, the outstanding Texas Ranger Museum, isn't far away, either. Waco, nicknamed Six-Shooter Junction in its early days, has a lot more going for it as a tourist center than most people realize, including its historic homes, which may be toured on weekends. The annual Brazos River Festival the last weekend in April, the Heart of Texas Fair in October, and the Great Texas Raft Race all attract thousands to this central Texas town. Explore it for yourself any time of the year, and make your stay more memorable at a B&B like this one.

1 bedroom, 1 bath
Moderate
No smoking. No pets.

Waxahachie

BBTS NO. 36

*S*carborough Faire, the medieval spring festival, and the Gingerbread Trail of Victorian homes each June draw thousands to Waxahachie each year. But don't wait for these events to visit this historic town, which is just off Interstate Highway 35 about thirty miles south of Dallas.

Staying at this delightful B&B with its fun-loving hosts is reason enough to make the pilgrimage here any time of the year. Built in 1920 and originally a manse for the Presbyterian Church, the house was bought by Bill and Charlene around twenty-six years ago. They added an enclosed L-shaped porch on one side in front, which accounts for the house's unusual shape. The gregarious couple obviously have green thumbs, for the porch is crammed full of flourishing plants. Guests sometimes like to eat breakfast amid the inviting oasis or relax at night by the light of a hundred-year-old lamp, a family treasure.

Their home reflects their frequent travels in this country and abroad, including a six-month stay in England, which "wasn't nearly long enough."

Among the mementos are framed brass rubbings from Westminster Abbey, which are on display in the breakfast nook for all to enjoy, along with brilliantly colored stained-glass panels—a red poppy and purple iris are two that have a lot of impact. The panels and all the other stained glass throughout the house were done by the talented artisan hosts, who take justifiable pride in their work.

Married about forty-three years, these childhood sweethearts have all kinds of interesting items around, like the skate key they shared when they were ten. A pair of gold earrings that had been given to his grandmother by an admirer when she was fifteen—a chief of police, no less—is also showcased in the hall.

The classy guest room has a double bed with an ivory spread, a couch and television set, an old-timey radio that still plays, a 1920 ceiling fan, and a private bath. Charlene needlepoints as she and her husband travel around the country in their motor home, and one of her pillows is on the bed. Since the room has its own entrance, you can come and go as you wish.

Sitting down to breakfast with guests is part of the fun, say the hosts, who serve a gourmet breakfast that includes strawberry soup (made from fresh strawberries) and a delicious egg and cheese casserole. Blueberry muffins are another treat you won't want to miss. They don't miss a trick in making everything extra special. Breakfast is served on white china with navy placemats, and a red bandana doubles as a napkin.

There are all kinds of inviting places to sit a spell in this comfortable B&B, especially in the backyard, which has a deck, a barbecue pit, and a lot of hanging baskets. Relax beneath a tall pecan or tulip tree and your cares will seem far away.

1 bedroom, 1 bath
Moderate
No smoking. No children.
No pets